Conservation and the Changing Direction of Economic Growth

Other Titles in This Series

Westview Special Studies in Natural Resources and Energy Management

Conservation and the Changing Direction of Economic Growth
edited by Bernhard J. Abrahamsson

The problem of energy resource scarcity is more related to financial and national security issues than to the availability of energy raw materials. This conclusion emerged from the June 1977 meeting of the Rocky Mountain Energy Economics Institute, which focused on the implications of the energy crisis for conservation and future economic growth in the U.S. This volume, based on six papers prepared for the June meeting, presents the view that, if flexibility of resource allocation is maintained, economic growth is not likely to come to a halt—at least not in the Western world. Conservation can achieve substantial energy savings, but conservation alone cannot solve the problem. Additional domestic supplies are needed, and coal is considered by many to be the main alternate domestic energy resource. These issues pose crucial questions for future policy vis-à-vis both economics and the environment.

Bernhard J. Abrahamsson is professor of international economic relations at the Graduate School of International Studies and senior research economist at the Denver Research Institute (DRI), both at the University of Denver. Dr. Abrahamsson is presently involved in research on U.S. natural gas consumption in his capacity as director of the Gas Requirements Agency of DRI. His writings have been published in several journals and he recently edited *The Changing Economics of World Energy* (Westview Press).

Published with the cooperation of the
Rocky Mountain Energy Economics Institute

Conservation and the Changing Direction of Economic Growth

edited by Bernhard J. Abrahamsson

Westview Press/Boulder, Colorado

Westview Special Studies in
Natural Resources and Energy Management

Published in 1978 in the United States of America by
    Westview Press, Inc.
    5500 Central Avenue
    Boulder, Colorado 80301
    Frederick A. Praeger, Publisher

Library of Congress Cataloging in Publication Data
Rocky Mountain Energy Economics Institute, 10th, Aspen, Colo., 1977.
    Conservation and the changing direction of economic growth.
    (Westview special studies in natural resources and energy management)
    Revisions of papers presented at the conference held June 26-29, 1977, and sponsored by the Rocky Mountain Oil and Gas Association and the Denver Research Institute.
    1. Energy policy—United States—Congresses. 2. Energy conservation—United States—Congresses. 3. United States—Economic policy—1971-   —Congresses. I. Abrahamsson, Bernhard J. II. Rocky Mountain Oil and Gas Association. III. Denver. University. Denver Research Institute. IV. Title.
HD9502.U52R62 1977   333.7   77-28753
ISBN 0-89158-029-8

Printed and bound in the United States of America

Contents

Figures and Tables

Preface

The chapters in this book were originally given as discussion papers at the 1977 Rocky Mountain Energy Economics Institute, sponsored by the Rocky Mountain Oil and Gas Association. The institute met in Aspen, Colorado, from June 26 to June 29, and, as in previous years, the program was planned and organized by Mr. Bob Burch, who also served as the moderator throughout the proceedings. Before publication in this volume, most papers were substantially revised.

The institute began as the Rocky Mountain Petroleum Economics Institute in 1963 at Mr. Burch's initiative. While the original intention was to schedule future institutes biennially, more frequent conferences have been held in response to needs and interest, and 1977 marks the tenth such meeting. Each institute has been planned, organized, and implemented by Mr. Burch; but from the very beginning, a regional academic institution has been invited to cosponsor the event and to publish the proceedings. The University of Denver, through the Denver Research Institute, has performed this function since 1971.

The institute brings together individuals from the energy industries, government, and academic circles. The group is intentionally kept small so that active participation is encouraged and so that each can benefit from the available individual expertise and accumulated experience. Formal papers are presented to express diverse perspectives and views and to stimulate discussion. No transcript is kept of the discussions, but the formal papers are published and made available to the public after the conference.

We wish to thank Helen Kneeland of the Rocky Mountain Oil and Gas Association and Lynne Roll of the Industrial Economics Division of the Denver Research Institute at the University of Denver for their assistance in the preparation of this work for publication.

The Contributors

Bernhard J. Abrahamsson, associate professor of international economic relations in the Graduate School of International Studies at the University of Denver and senior research economist at the University of Denver Research Institute, brings to the reader a wide perspective on the economics of world energy. In his capacity as director of the Gas Requirement Agency at the institute, Dr. Abrahamsson is currently involved in research on U.S. natural gas consumption. He has done extensive research on oil in the context of international shipping and in 1974 coauthored *Strategic Aspects of Seaborne Oil.* Among his many professional activities, he has served on the staff of the International Monetary Fund, taught at the Universities of Alaska and Haifa, and served as scientific director and advisor to the Israel Shipping Research Institute. He is an active member of the Ocean Policy Committee of the National Research Council's Commission on International Relations.

Edward W. Erickson is professor of economics and business at North Carolina State University. He has written numerous articles on energy issues and policies and has testified on energy matters before many congressional committees. Professor Erickson was staff consultant to the Cabinet Task Force on Oil Import Controls (1969-1970) and chairman of the Technical-Supply Advisory Committee on Exploration,

Development, and New Reserves Additions for the NPC Natural Gas Survey (1975-1976). He has also been a member of the National Petroleum Council and the North Carolina Energy Policy Council, and has participated in international as well as domestic symposia on energy.

Herbert S. Winokur, Jr., is vice-president for energy planning and development at the Pennsylvania Company. He holds a Ph.D. in economics and statistics from Harvard University, where he also teaches. Dr. Winokur has written extensively on energy and policy issues and has served both industry and government—notably the Cabinet Task Force on Oil Import Controls—in executive and consulting capacities.

James W. McKie is professor of economics at the University of Texas at Austin. He specializes in, and has published prolifically in, the fields of energy economics, industrial organization, and the economics of government regulation. Professor McKie has served as senior fellow of the Brookings Institution and as a member of President Johnson's Antitrust Task Force, the National Science Foundation's Advisory Committee on Environmental Sciences, and the Cabinet Task Force on Oil Import Controls. Currently, he is affiliated with the American Enterprise Institute.

Joel Darmstadter is an economist and fellow with Resources for the Future (RFF) in Washington, D.C. He holds degrees from The George Washington University and the graduate faculty of the New School for Social Research. Mr. Darmstadter is the author or coauthor of a number of RFF books on energy, has contributed widely to professional journals, and has lectured before academic, scientific, and public interest groups. He has testified before congressional committees and served in an advisory capacity to a number of government bodies.

L. G. Rawl is executive vice-president and a member of the management committee of Exxon USA. He is a graduate of the University of Oklahoma and joined Exxon in 1952 as a petroleum engineer. He served in 1967-69 as executive assistant to the chairman of the board of Exxon Corporation. He became a senior vice-president in 1972 and executive vice-president in 1976. A registered professional engineer, he is a member of the Society of Petroleum Engineers, the American Petroleum Institute, the board of directors for the Houston Chamber of Commerce, and the executive committee of the Natural Gas Supply Committee.

Richard L. Gordon is professor of mineral economics at Pennsylvania State University, where he is involved in his department's broad program of teaching and research on the economic analysis of mineral industries' problems. Professor Gordon has written extensively on coal economics as well as on energy and mineral policy in general, and on the pure theory of the optimal exploitation of exhaustible resources. He has been the chairman of the Council of Economics of the American Institute of Mining, Metallurgical, and Petroleum Engineers. He has served in a consulting capacity to the Federal Energy Administration, National Science Foundation, U.S. Department of Justice, and several industrial and consulting firms.

Milton Lipton is executive vice-president of W. J. Levy Consultants Corporation, and has been lecturer and adjunct professor of economics at several universities, including the University of California and New York University. He has been associated with the National Bureau of Economic Research, the Conference Board, the Business Research Advisory Committee, U.S. Bureau of Labor Statistics, and the Wealth Inventory Planning Study. Mr. Lipton is the author and coauthor of numerous articles, reviews, and monographs on petroleum economics, energy, productivity, and investment decision making.

Abbreviations

AGA	American Gas Association
b/d	barrels per day
Btu	British thermal unit
c.i.f.	cost, insurance, and freight
COMECON	Council for Mutual Economic Assistance
EIS	environmental impact statement
EPA	Environmental Protection Agency
ERDA	Energy Research and Development Administration
FEA	Federal Energy Administration
FPC	Federal Power Commission
GDP	gross domestic product
GNP	gross national product
LDC	less-developed country
LNG	liquefied natural gas
Mcf	thousand cubic feet
mb/d	thousands of barrels per day
mmb/d	millions of barrels per day
mmb/doe	millions of barrels per day oil equivalent
mmt	million tons
mpg	miles per gallon
NPC	National Petroleum Council
NPR	naval petroleum reserve
OCS	Outer Continental Shelf

oe	oil equivalent
OECD	Organization for Economic Cooperation and Development
OPEC	Organization of Petroleum Exporting Countries
R&D	research and development
SNG	synthetic natural gas
tcf	trillion cubic feet

Introduction

Bernhard J. Abrahamsson

The 1977 Rocky Mountain Energy Economics Institute took place at a time when the need for a national energy plan had reached the very top of social priorities. The Carter administration had presented its national energy plan in April 1977, and, following the institute's tradition of focusing on timely, policy-oriented topics, the discussions centered on the two key elements of the plan: conservation and extensive conversion to coal use.[1]

There is a substantial difference between the present plan and those proposed by previous administrations beginning with President Nixon's energy message in June 1971. Although energy conservation and extended use of coal did play a role in the policy statements made by Nixon and Ford, the main thrust, prompted by national security considerations, was to decrease our oil import dependence by developing domestic supplies of all kinds of energy. Implied in this approach was an optimistic view of the physical availability of both domestic and foreign fuel resources. The Carter plan, by contrast, is intended to cope with the consequences of a perceived global depletion of energy resources. It is undoubtedly a view derived, at least in part, from the lessons learned from Project Independence.

It is a truism to say that the world's resources are finite and that, therefore, we will eventually face a physical scarcity of fuels. The real question is when. There are several studies of this question. One interesting study of international scope is the report of the MIT Workshop on Alternative Energy Strategies (WAES), which foresees such a scarcity sometime between 1981-2004 under all reasonable scenarios of economic growth, price, and government policy.[2] Of particular interest, however, is a Central Intelligence Agency (CIA) report that appears to have had substantial influence in shaping the views of the Carter administration. This report, which Erickson and Winokur review extensively in Chapter 1, sees a global scarcity already by 1985.

Historically, forecasts of this kind have been wrong, because they require assumptions about too many and too complex political, economic, social, technological, and recently, environmental developments.

The simple truth is that we do not know where the resource limits are. If we follow the historical pattern of resource utilization, we will first run out of easily accessible and, therefore, cheap energy. As less accessible, high-cost resources are brought into use, we move into eras of progressively more expensive energy. Although technological progress will offset such cost increases, we do not know to what extent, when, or for how long it will do so.

The conclusion of the institute left a strong impression that our knowledge is, indeed, incomplete. The participants, representing industry, government, and academe, responded to the issues in terms of their own particular specialties and perspectives. There clearly were gaps in the understanding of interactions among the economic, political, and technological processes and relationships that seem to be moving us increasingly toward a situation where most obstacles to man's conquest of nature are not found in nature itself but in man-made institutions.

Undoubtedly, physical depletion of resources will occur sometime, but the predominant argument at the institute was that at present, the root of the energy problem is lack of appropriate economic incentives rather than a physical short-age. This theme is developed in Chapter 1, which also shows how sensitive forecasts are to changed assumptions. The authors, E. W. Erickson and H. S. Winokur, Jr., argue that the energy "crisis" is primarily financial, with both short-term and long-term aspects. In the short term, the world's econo-mies are faced with the problems of adjustment as energy be-comes relatively more expensive. The longer-term aspect involves the type of adjustment and the rate at which it is achieved in the United States relative to the rest of the world. It is on this long-term aspect that Chapter 1 focuses, because, unless appropriate policies are pursued, the financial crisis can easily spiral into a real crisis. The authors take issue with the administration's current policies—particularly the lack of incentives for supply creation and the reliance on regulation and standards to replace individual investment decisions—because the fundamental premises about supply and demand management from which these policies derive are incorrect. It is very important to recognize that Western Hemisphere oil and gas supply is very dependent on public policy decisions concerning tax and price incentives.

Since the current "crisis" thinking appears to draw much upon the CIA report published in April 1977, that report is subjected to an exhaustive analysis. It is shown that for the period until 1980, the report presents views similar to those given in the 1969 Cabinet Task Force Report. Both reports agree that no "crisis" is looming in the next few years, but the CIA report sees such a crisis by 1985. However, that con-clusion is dependent on crucial assumptions about demand and supply developments in particularly the United States, the Soviet Union, and the Western Hemisphere. Well-reasoned changes in these assumptions remove the catastrophic conclu-sions of the CIA's report and clearly show an alternative focus for U.S. energy policy. In general, policies that increase the U.S. supply base are likely to have great effects in the world markets as well. In particular, deregulation of natural gas is expected to have marked effects on supply and to reduce the U.S. incremental demand for imported oil; this, in turn, will reduce pressures on world oil prices. The overall long-term outcomes of domestic U.S. energy policies will thus have major economic and political consequences.

But wrong forecasts in the past do not necessarily mean they will be wrong again. What may happen to the U.S. economy if there are substantial scarcities? This is the question to which Professor McKie turns. Continuing the longer-term focus from the first chapter, he looks at the consequences for the United States of high energy prices. The specific questions are whether economic growth can continue or whether even the present levels of output and employment can be sustained as energy becomes scarcer and costlier.

To answer these questions—and for the sake of argument —the author assumes that the current pessimistic projections for energy are correct. That is, we are rapidly running out of hydrocarbons, and there is little prospect of finding more; the cost of alternatives will be higher than in the past; and technologies of potential substitutes will be slow to develop. What will happen under these circumstances?

As energy supplies become scarcer and costlier, economic growth must be constrained, because our energy-intensive economy must, first, use less energy and, second, devote more resources to the production of energy. These resources could have provided other valuable goods and services. The economic problem is how the economy reacts to this higher *real* cost of energy. The ensuing analysis makes several noteworthy points. Since energy is a produced good, its availability depends—through the process of investment in the energy industries—on its price. Moreover, energy is an input in the production process and can therefore be replaced by nonenergy inputs; and as energy-intensive goods and services become more expensive, substitution by other goods and services will occur. In addition, technology will progress along energy-saving tracks. Furthermore, as conventional oil and gas supplies become scarcer and costlier, coal, nuclear, and solar energy will provide "backstops" for the economy's energy needs. Energy will be more expensive, but we are not likely to run out of it.

This general conclusion is further amplified by three models, which are summarized at the end of the chapter. Each model considers the process of growth in relation to energy supplies derived from investment in energy production constrained by resource endowments. Incorporating technological change and growth in the labor supply, the models indicate only small effects on long-term economic growth. Of particular interest is the finding that employment does not depend on cheap energy if the economy has time to adjust. Although this does not mean that the future is free of problems and questions, it does show that adjustment is highly dependent on political factors and has an international dimension as well.

In the first two chapters, the analysis implies that conservation of energy is achieved primarily through the price mechanism. But conservation is not as unambiguous a concept as commonly thought. It can be applied to both the demand for and supply of energy. Indeed, it is in the conservation of their resource that Organization of Petroleum Exporting Countries (OPEC) members may manifest their power and precipitate a supply shortage. If applied to the demand side, conservation can result from the price mechanism, a change in social behavior, or from technological changes. The Carter plan explicitly intends to steer us toward conservation on the demand side. Support for such measures is often found in the popular debate by comparing the ratio of energy consumption to gross national product (GNP) of, particularly, Sweden and Germany to that of the United States. Do energy consumption patterns abroad, and their implied conservation measures, provide guidelines for U.S. policy? J. Darmstadter explores this question in Chapter 3. Specifically, he examines the factors accounting for differences in energy consumption in several industrial countries whose per capita GNPs are comparable. The energy-output ratio of the United States is compared to that of eight other industrial countries. The analysis shows that there are complex and diverse reasons for intercountry differences in energy consumption. Although there is scope for changing the pattern of U.S. energy use, variations in the energy-output ratios should not in themselves be viewed as indicators of economic efficiency, or even of energy efficiency. Economic efficiency depends on how energy is used in combination with other resources and on the relative costs of all of these. National energy-output ratios also depend critically on the composition of a country's output, not merely on the energy intensities associated with these component products and activities. If we want to change the pattern of U.S. energy use, it seems that more appropriate economic signals to energy users must be a key factor. Darmstadter finds that energy consumption is essentially only one element of societal arrangements and choices, and it may have considerable use flexibility. It is simplistic, and at odds with the facts, to assume that there exists abroad an energy conservation ethic entirely lacking in the United States. Such thinking diverts from the urgent task of formulating conservation strategies appropriate to this country.

While Darmstadter looks at general relationships and possibilities for U.S. conservation policies, L. H. Rawl, in Chapter 4, focuses on the nation's specific potentials for conservation and increased supplies of energy. Drawing upon the Exxon Corporation's *Energy Outlook* (February 1977), he forecasts a slowing of growth rates in all major categories of energy consumption. The slowdown leads to a "saving," or conservation, of almost 18 million barrels per day (mmb/d) by 1990 over what consumption would have been with historical rates. But this saving is contingent on substantial realization of the *technical potential* for conservation in the various use categories.

Although these projected "savings" are larger than the total U.S. oil consumption in 1976, the U.S. energy demand in 1990 is expected to reach the equivalent of 54 million barrels of oil per day. Hence, supplies of energy must increase substantially during this period. On the assumption that environmental constraints will be appropriately adjusted and that policies will encourage a vigorous development of energy sources, the author projects rapid growth in nuclear and coal energy. The latter source is expected to be of particular importance for industries and utilities. However, there are economic and technical limits to industry's change from oil and gas to coal. Therefore, oil and gas will still provide the bulk of U.S. energy requirements even beyond 1990. These oil and gas supplies must come from production from existing reserves, synthetics, new domestic discoveries, or imports. Of these, only the last two sources offer prospects for increased supplies. Since the main reliance is now already on imports, it is necessary to have a rapid and aggressive program of domestic exploration and development to change the situation in the future.

It is clear that conservation, however caused, will not be sufficient to meet the supply-demand gap foreseen in the National Energy Plan. Therefore, expanded use of coal is one of the keystones of the Carter administration's proposed long-term energy policy, and the conclusions in Chapter 4 depend critically on such expansion. But is it realistic to count on expanded coal use? In Chapter 5, R. Gordon examines this question, or, as he phrases it, the "coal schizophrenia" of energy policy. This is the "proclivity to make resounding pronouncements about the need to increase U.S. coal prodution significantly and then impose regulations severely limiting coal production and use."

For Gordon, the answer to the energy problem does not lie in any single action or resource. Although it is of course necessary, conservation is not a question of moral fiber but one of improper price signals caused by regulation, particu-

larly on oil and gas. The response of both demand and supply to
price signals is likely to be much greater than expected. It is
much the same with coal. Coal should play a significant role
in our future energy picture, but it is unrealistic to expect us
to move toward a predominantly coal-based economy.

On the supply side of coal, there are serious questions
about the resource base itself, its quality, location, and
potential for expanded production. Other questions and
problems relate to production costs, transportation, and
technology. Institutional barriers are found in environmental
constraints and in complex state and federal regulations that
impede the acquisition of mining rights and the securing of
permits to operate a mine.

On the demand side, there are problems of public opposition to both expanded production and use, as well as the uncertain financial position of electric utilities. The technology to
comply with clean air standards is costly and appears unreli-
able, yet industry conversions to coal are increasingly
mandated by the federal govenment. In addition, except for
utilities, industry has a very small potential for conversion,
and mandated conversion seems to be one of the least efficient ways of promoting the use of coal.

On balance, Gordon feels that the administration's approach to a national energy policy is to seek increases in coal
use that may simply be too large to be effected under current
regulatory procedures. At the same time, these procedures
are becoming more, rather than less, complicated—hence,
"coal schizophrenia."

When all is said and done, what then can government
policy accomplish? In the final chapter, Milton Lipton turns
to this question and considers the critical choices that must
be made for a national energy policy. The success of such a
policy depends entirely on the making, and determined pur-
suit, of correct choices. But there is much difficulty and uncertainty, because policymaking is a dynamic process of con-
ciliation of market forces and political objectives, which are

often imprecise and change with circumstances.

Recognizing these difficulties, Lipton sees the major policy concerns and critical choices as centered in five areas. The first—on which he does not dwell—is the building of a *strategic petroleum reserve.* Other areas are *domestic* oil and gas prices, *energy conservation, coal conversion,* and *research and development* for alternative energy sources.

Essentially, today's policy in these areas will build a bridge to the future, when research and development (R&D) will provide alternative resources and technologies. Industry will almost inevitably have the responsibility for R&D, because it has the needed capabilities and diversity of perspectives. But industry must also have adequate incentives, and these must be provided by government policy—otherwise "energy policy could turn out to have been a bridge to nowhere."

The issue of domestic oil and gas prices is pivotal to any policy and seriously affects both conservation and conversion. Conservation is an urgent issue because price elasticities of demand for various energy sources are uncertain. To shift from increasingly scarce oil and gas to abundant coal seems to be a clear policy direction; but there is conflict focused on environmental, economic, and regional interests.

The present dilemma, with respect to domestic oil and gas prices, is how to formulate policy when regulated prices are based on historical costs while the need is now to provide price incentives for future energy developments. This dilemma stems from the fact that the world price of oil is a political price. The large difference between OPEC costs and prices gives rise to a "political rent" exacted by OPEC. This price becomes the reference point for the current value of oil in the United States and elsewhere, and the difference between this current value and historical costs creates an "economic rent," which is subject to competing claims from producers, consumers, and government.

One alternative to the dilemma is deregulation, but this

would simply mean that OPEC, rather than the U.S. government, will administer domestic prices. The situation is improved if deregulation is coupled wtih excess profits taxes.
Although there are arguments for this solution, Lipton feels
it entails too many uncertain political ramifications. Instead,
he suggests "incentive pricing." This can be done by control-
ling *new oil* at the necessary incentive price and keeping the
old oil price for established production. The volume subjected to the old price would be progressively reduced until
old oil is phased out and one incentive price exists in the
domestic market. The argument behind this price policy is
that the OPEC price is irrelevant for U.S. energy policy. The
important aspect of domestic policy is that industry should
be able to anticipate with confidence the trend in domestic
prices so that an expanded exploration effort can be predicted to bridge us to future alternatives.

As the chapters in this book illustrate, the basic problem
can be stated simply. There may be an energy supply-demand
gap, at least for some time, regardless of whether the supply
constraint is physical or political. Because of adjustment
problems and time lags in investments and R&D, oil and gas
will remain the major fuels in the immediate future. Under
existing regulatory conditions and with declining domestic
production of these fuels, we have become increasingly dependent on foreign sources—a development expected to continue in the future.

The general solution to the problem can be stated in
equally simple terms. The more energy we produce and the
less we consume, the less dependent we will be on foreign
sources and vulnerable supply lines. Hence, the less subject
we will be to political coercion and balance-of-payments
problems.

It is the formulation of specific policy measures that
causes problems. We are laboring under conditions where the
only certainty is uncertainty about basic international and
domestic facts. Too little is known about the resource bases

and the responsiveness of supply and demand to changes in the prices of various sources of energy. Not only have we paid scant attention to the physical nature and location of coal—our most abundant energy resource—but we have paid even less attention to the many institutional problems in this sector. These problems also exist with regard to the outer continental shelf as well as in the traditional areas of oil and gas exploration. Technologically, we may be on the threshold of major breakthroughs to unlock new, but known, sources of oil and gas and to tap the so-called exotic sources of energy.

Under such circumstances, our policies should be flexible and responsive as we gain further knowledge and new developments unfold. Energy may never again be as inexpensive as in the past, but with proper policies we may obtain an acceptable trade-off between energy price and national vulnerability. To establish what constitutes such policies and trade-offs requires informed debate and judgment. We hope this book contributes to this end.

Notes

1. See Appendix B for a summary of the National Energy Plan.
2. Carroll L. Wilson, *Energy: Global Prospects, 1985-2000* (New York: McGraw-Hill, 1977).

1
World Oil and Gas Supply: Whose Crisis?

Edward W. Erickson and
Herbert S. Winokur, Jr.

The outlook for world oil and gas supply and price is both as confused and as extensively debated as any current topic. On the one hand, our civilization is every so often said to be "running out of energy"; for the last hundred years, it has especially been "running out of oil." Each of these forecasts has proven to be untrue, either because we, in responding to the pressures related to supply and demand, found a more economic substitute (as the price of the scarce resource increased) or because we simply have found more oil than was previously thought could be produced. It is tempting, therefore, to assume that the current "energy crisis" is just the outgrowth of another pessimistic forecast and should not be taken seriously.

On the other hand, substantial temerity is required to ignore the "conventional wisdom" offered by such authorities as the Central Intelligence Agency, major oil companies, and the president of the United States. Each of these authorities correctly notes that continued geometric demand growth, even at less than historical rates, offset only by arithmetic supply increases, will lead ultimately to an "excess of demand over supply" and hence to substantially higher prices.[1] This chapter attempts to reconcile these disparate perspectives by discussing some of the key issues that affect the outlook for world oil and gas supply over the next ten to fifteen years.

By way of introduction, it is amusing to explore at least one writer's perspective about the energy crisis. Lewis Lapham, writing in *Harper's,* notes that he has been deluged over the last several years with articles, papers, memorandums, and government reports about the "energy crisis."[2] Although he admits that he is unable (at the current writing) to identify exactly what the energy crisis is (he calls it an "unparalleled misfortune that exists, if it exists at all, at an imaginary point where six or seven lines intersect on a graph"), he has been able to identify three of the important properties of this "crisis."

First, he notes that "the crisis has yet to achieve palpable form." It may be "a cataclysm of no doubt wondrous magnificence," but it is "as yet undiscovered and abstract." According to some authors (e.g., the CIA), Lapham notes, it will appear in four or five years; according to other authors, in ten to twenty years.

Second, "the crisis has to do with money, not with raw materials." Even the doomsayers agree that there is an abundance of oil and gas (and coal), enough to last for many years, but that the recovery of these resources will be both socially and financially expensive. Definition of the "crisis" in this fashion is difficult, particularly in public presentation: the "moral equivalent of war" is a question of money. The ambiguity surrounding the crisis even in Washington creates substantial public confusion. No wonder, then, that about half of those interviewed in a recent Gallup poll did not know that the United States is heavily dependent on imported oil to meet its energy needs; fewer than half of those interviewed in a Roper poll agreed that the oil "shortage" is real and the "problem" will get worse.[3]

Third, "the crisis appears much more terrifying to the rich than to the poor." Lapham points out that the poor paid little attention to the crisis, perhaps because they have little need to worry about heating ski lodges or operating a multitude of household appliances: "Among the affluent classes

. . . the news of the crisis carried the weight of Biblical judgment. . . . That the energy crisis should weigh so heavily on the minds of the rich seems to me consistent with its chimerical nature. Only the rich can afford to be so frightened of things unseen.''

In our view, this summary of the so-called energy crisis is accurate as well as entertaining. But the ''crisis'' does contain real elements. It also has both short-run and long-run aspects. Its short-term aspect involves the adjustment of the U.S. (and world) economy to the change in relative prices (and thus to the change in political consequences) as energy becomes relatively more expensive. The longer-term aspect of the ''crisis'' involves the adjustment of the U.S. economy to new long-term energy supply/price relationships, *relative to* the world economy. Paradoxically, in the latter adjustment energy may become both more readily available and, perhaps, more secure to the United States than to many of its industrialized or developing trading partners. Such developments depend upon the relative positions of coal, oil, gas, and uranium in the world energy market and also upon the pattern of intercountry trade flows.

This chapter presents a critique of the CIA's recent oil supply/demand forecast, with special emphasis on CIA assumptions about Soviet and Western Hemisphere oil supply and U.S. natural gas supply (and its effects on oil demand). After this critique, the chapter concludes by listing some of the political issues that will affect the pace of the adjustments mentioned above. In each topic treated, the political issues appear overwhelming.

The CIA Report: A Gloomy "Forecast"

The CIA's recently published ''The International Energy Situation: Outlook to 1985'' has been quoted frequently in the press.[4] The official stature awarded this forecast and its dismal outlook merit our special scrutiny.

TABLE 1.1

Oil Demand and Supply Projections

(Millions of barrels per day)

	1976	1980
Free World Oil Demand	48.4	54.9 - 56.7
United States	16.7	19.3 - 20.7
OECD Europe	13.6	13.7 - 14.7
Japan	5.2	6.2 - 6.6
Canada	2.0	2.2 - 2.4
Other developed countries[1]	1.2	1.4
Non-OPEC LDCs	6.7	8.5
OPEC countries	2.1	3.0
Other Demand[2]	0.9	0
Non-OPEC supply[3]	17.5	22.0
United States	9.7	10.0
OECD Europe	0.9	3.7
Japan	0	0
Canada	1.6	1.5
Other developed countries[1]	0.5	0.5
Non-OPEC LDCs	3.7	6.1
Net Communist trade		
USSR-Eastern Europe	0.9	-0.3
China	0.2	0.5
Required OPEC production	30.9	32.9 - 34.7

NOTES:

(1) Australia, Israel, New Zealand, and South Africa.
(2) Including stock changes and statistical discrepancy.
(3) Including natural gas liquids.

We want to demonstrate two conclusions. First, the 1980 forecasts of world and U.S. supply and demand are not new—in fact they almost exactly parallel government forecasts made nine years ago. Second, the forecasts for 1985 are extraordinarily sensitive to a few and somewhat questionable assumptions, so sensitive that small changes in individual assumptions substantially weaken the report's general conclusions.[5]

Table 1.1 shows the recent CIA forecast for U.S. and world oil supply and demand in 1980, and a comparison with 1976 actual data.[6] For 1980, the CIA projects a world demand for oil of approximately 55 million barrels per day

TABLE 1.2

World Demand and Production, 1980

(Millions of barrels per day)

Total Demand:	Total Production	United States	Canada	Other
Western Hemisphere:				
United States	11.0	11.0	M	M
Canada	4.5	3.0	1.5	M
Other	8.2	3.8	0.4	4.0
Eastern Hemisphere:				
Arab	28.9	1.4	0.1	27.4
Free non-Arab	7.2	0.5	M	6.7
Soviet bloc net exports	0.8	M	M	0.8
Total Demand	60.6	19.7	2.0	38.9

NOTES:

(1) Soviet bloc exports represent gross exports of 1.8 mmb/d in 1980, reduced by gross imports of 1.0 mmb/d in 1980, in accordance with information supplied by the Department of the Interior staff.

(2) M = minimal.

SOURCE:

The Oil Import Question, p. 49.

(mmb/d), with OPEC production of about 34 mmb/d. The United States is expected to consume approximately 20 mmb/d and to supply about half of that, or about 10 mmb/d. It is also interesting to note that the "required" OPEC production forecast for 1980 of about 34 mmb/d exceeds the 1976 OPEC production by only about 10 percent.

Comparison of the CIA Report to Earlier Forecasts

The report of the Cabinet Task Force on Oil Import Control, prepared in 1969-1970, forecasts both world and U.S. oil supply and demand for 1980 (Table 1.2).[7] These forecasts were based on projections submitted by major and independent oil companies, government bodies, and nonoil industrial groups.

The Cabinet Task Force forecast approximately 60 mmb/d of free world oil demand in 1980, or about 8 percent higher than the demand forecast by the CIA. (Presumably the substantial increase in real price since 1970 has had some effect on demand, even if the Cabinet Task Force forecast had been exactly right. Or one could argue that the price increases had little effect on demand, and the discrepancy represents simply forecast error; or that 1980 demand at the prices then foreseen would have been much higher than the task force predicted and that it is only coincidental that 1980 demand as forecast by the CIA approximates the task force's forecast.)

The similarity in forecast results for the United States is even more striking. The Cabinet Task Force forecast of 20 mmb/d of 1980 U.S. oil demand is precisely the midpoint of the CIA forecast, implying that price controls have cushioned the full effect that world oil price increases have had on U.S. demand. Further, the forecast for U.S. supply at different prices prepared by the Cabinet Task Force covered the range of 9.5 to 13.5 mmb/d; the CIA forecast lies within that range, although toward the lower end. One of the reasons we think that supply has not reached previous expectations is that federal price control programs have created perverse incentives; the present price of "old oil" in the United States is below 1969-1970 levels after adjustment for inflation and changes in tax laws.[8] Another reason is that leasing programs have suffered serious delays.

For whatever reasons, both the CIA forecast and the Cabinet Task Force forecast present similar views on 1980 world oil supply and demand.[9] The supply/demand balance will not be terribly different from what was foreseen nearly a decade ago—although prices are substantially higher than in previous forecasts—and now as then, no crisis is predicted for 1980.

The CIA Forecast for 1985

For 1985, the consequences of the CIA forecast become

TABLE 1.3

Oil Demand and Supply Projections

(Millions of barrels per day)

	1976	1985
Free World Oil Demand	48.4	68.3 - 72.6
United States	16.7	22.2 - 25.6
OECD Europe	13.6	15.8 - 18.2
Japan	5.2	8.1 - 8.8
Canada	2.0	2.9 - 3.5
Other developed countries[1]	1.2	1.9
Non-OPEC LDCs	6.7	12.0
OPEC countries	2.1	4.0
Other Demand[2]	0.9	0
Non-OPEC supply[3]	17.5	20.4 - 22.4
United States	9.7	10.0 - 11.0
OECD Europe	0.9	4.0 - 5.0
Japan	0	0.1
Canada	1.6	1.3 - 1.5
Other developed countries[1]	0.5	0.4
Non-OPEC LDCs	3.7	8.0 - 9.0
Net Communist trade USSR-Eastern Europe China	0.9	-3.5 - -4.5
Required OPEC production	30.9	46.7 - 51.2

NOTES:

(1) Australia, Israel, New Zealand, and South Africa.
(2) Including stock changes and statistical discrepancy.
(3) Including natural gas liquids.

SOURCE:

CIA, p. 15.

alarming, as Table 1.3 shows. Demand is projected to escalate rapidly, from 55 mmb/d in 1980 to approximately 70 mmb/d in 1985 (or about 5 percent per year) while non-OPEC supply remains roughly constant. In addition, the Soviet Union/Eastern European bloc is projected to move from a state of approximate internal supply/demand balance to a state that requires imports of 4 mmb/d of OPEC production. Required OPEC production, therefore, increases from about 34 mmb/d to as much as 51 mmb/d by 1985.

Since the only substantial excess capacity remaining is generally agreed to be that of Saudi Arabia, the question is whether Saudi Arabia either can or will be willing to increase its production at the required rate. The CIA report suggests that "by 1982 or 1983, sizable price increases are inevitable unless large-scale conservation measures cut demand sharply," reasoning that although the Saudis have the reserves necessary to support the required level of production, there is considerable doubt that the Saudis can or will complete such an expansion program.

We concur that for the foreseeable future, the Saudis hold the key to both substantial new supply and price.[10] For the sake of argument, we will also accept as given the CIA demand forecasts.[11] But we would question the doomsday forecast of the CIA—for three reasons. First, we think it is unlikely that the Soviet Union and Eastern Europe will import so much OPEC oil. Second, we think that potential production in the Western Hemisphere, particularly the proposed outputs from Venezuelan and Canadian heavy oil projects, could add an additional 2 mmb/d of output by 1984, even at current real prices. Third, we think that appropriate government policy in the United States could increase U.S. oil and gas supply by as much as 20 percent over that forecast by the CIA.

Small changes in assumptions in these three areas would together have a significant effect on the 1985 world oil supply and demand balance. These assumptions do not have to do with geology or the existence of the resource base itself. Rather, they have to do with the future behavior of national and international organizations, in particular with the economic and political environments these organizations create. And the behavioral effect is extremely significant.

Soviet Oil and Gas

There is now a substantial interest in Soviet oil and gas

development. Much of this interest has resulted from claims of large-scale reserves and production possibilities in the Soviet Union.

The Soviet Resource Base

The consensus of the forecasts reviewed here is that both the geography and the geology support the enormous oil and gas reserve potential that the USSR is expected to have.[12] For example, West Siberia has a sedimentary basin that has approximately five times the surface area of either France or Texas. Nearly half of the Soviet Union's subsoil comprises the sedimentary structures that are most interesting to oil geologists. The Soviet Union contains 37 percent of the world's sedimentary areas; by contrast, the Near and Middle East has 11 percent and North America only 2 percent.

The potential therefore seems enormous, for both oil and gas, in terms of both proved and probable reserves. Experts estimate total West Siberian oil production to be nearly 200 billion tons, or 1.4 trillion barrels, during the whole exploitation period.[13] By way of reference, this amount approximates 200 years of present U.S. oil consumption.

The Soviet Prospects for 1985

Table 1.4, with some simple linear extrapolation, indicates the sensitivity of the assumptions underlying the CIA forecast and suggests that the Soviet Union/Eastern European bloc may well continue to balance internal oil supply and demand.

Soviet Supply Problems

The key factor, therefore, is less one of finding oil in the ground, and more one of creating the infrastructures in the crude-bearing regions. These infrastructures must be developed in terrible climatic conditions, even worse than those faced in the construction of the Trans-Alaskan pipeline. In addition, the construction of the transportation system itself will be very complex and expensive. As has often been noted, distance is Russia's plight.

But even at today's prices, exploitation appears to be profitable. A recent study estimates that $2.50 to $3.50 per barrel production costs, and similar transportation costs, would be adequate to permit West Siberia's output to be delivered to Europe (ex tax), compared with the approximately $12 to $13 per barrel c.i.f. price of OPEC oil delivered to Europe.[14] The major immediate problem—given a decision to proceed with substantial development—appears to be the availability of hard currency to purchase technology and equipment in adequate quantity (for example, sufficient quantities of large-diameter pipe). But as the Soviets become more integrated into world product and capital markets, a Soviet decision to proceed could be the basis for a project-financing arrangement that would solve such a problem.

For example, major Soviet gas exports to Western Europe are forecast to increase significantly by 1980 and beyond. Western European imports of Soviet gas could increase from 8 billion cubic meters in 1975 to 23 billion cubic meters by 1980. Several Soviet gas fields are at least as large as the immense Groningen field in Holland.[15] Participation by Western countries in capital investment projects related to these gas exports will free the Soviet Union's internal resources for other uses and allow it to import technology and hard currency for other projects, such as the oil projects necessary to continue Soviet bloc self-sufficiency. On the other hand, the expansion of Soviet gas (and oil) exports, with attendant pipeline links, could significantly shift perceptions about European, U.S., and OECD security and its relation to energy "self-sufficiency."

All the studies cited here agree that the Soviets could, but probably will not choose to, gear up their industrial structure to export significant amounts of oil into the world oil market in the 1980s. But although those studies do not conclude that net oil output will jump enormously, there appear to be

TABLE 1.4

Oil Balance of COMECON Countries

(Million tons/year)

	1970	1973	1974	1975	Prospects 1980	Prospects 1985 A	Prospects 1985 B
USSR							
Production	353	427	459	490	620-640	680-700	770
Consumption (incl. losses & stocks)	257.2	308.7	342.8	359.7	520	730	630
Balance exports	95.8	118.3	116.2	130.3	100-120	30-(50)	140
OTHER EAST EUROPEAN COUNTRIES[1]							
Production	16.3	17.1	17.4	17.5	20	20	20
Consumption (incl. losses & stock changes)	61	84	87.7	93	120-140	168-196	146-170
Net Imports	44.7	66.9	70.3	75.5	100-120	148-176	126-150
(of which from USSR)	40.3	55.2	58.7	64	80	NA	NA
Net Balance COMECON Exports	51.1	51.4	45.9	54.8	About 0	(178)-(216)	14-(10)

NOTES:

(1) Excluding Yugoslavia and Albania.

Oil products in tons of crude, on the basis of: 1 ton crude = 0.92 ton of oil products. 10 million tons/year = approximately 0.2 mmb/d.

Figures within parentheses indicate negative numbers.

SOURCE:

Total Information, Tables I and II. 1985 estimates are prepared by the authors. The first 1985 estimate, which is similar to that presented by the CIA, assumes continued 7 percent per annum (p.a.) consumption growth, and only a 10 percent total increase in supply over projected 1980 levels as previously predicted by the Soviets in 1972. The second estimate assumes growth in demand of 4 percent p.a., while supply increases between 1980 and 1985 in the same absolute amount as it is projected to do between 1975 and 1980.

strong political, geologic, and economic reasons why the Eastern European/Soviet bloc will not become a significant importer by 1985, as forecast by the CIA.

Western Hemisphere Supply

Heavy Oils

Production from heavy-oil deposits in Canada and Venezuela, even though development is expected to proceed relatively slowly, could run as high as 2 mmb/d by 1985 according to recent trade press articles. Published cost estimates for Venezuelan heavy oil run about $8 per barrel before refining and transportation, or about the cost of North Sea oil.[16]

New Areas

Although the CIA report explicitly considers Mexican oil and gas, it pays little attention to potential supply from other parts of Central and South America. Some industry forecasts show large production potential in these areas; however, the potential has not been realized, in large part for political reasons. Successful exploration has not been well rewarded in these areas. But we feel direct approaches to the risk-sharing "problem," as discussed later, could supplement heavy-oil production and add 2 mmb/d altogether to Western Hemisphere output by 1985.

Public Policy Issues Affecting Supply

The Athabasca tar sands in Alberta, Canada, are well known to contain many billions of barrels of oil. It is also well known that the technical processes exist to recover this oil. What is not well known is the economic viability of the recovery processes. In the past, this economic uncertainty arose from two sources: (1) the world price of oil, which established the Athabasca netback; and (2) the tax treatment of tar sand output.

One of those uncertainties—sufficiently high world oil prices—has now been removed, and in terms of netback prices covering the real resource costs of extraction, tar sand production is clearly on the verge of being economic. The tax treatment question is perhaps now being resolved. But the Athabascan tar sands experience illustrates an important point: namely, that Western Hemisphere oil and gas supply is very dependent upon public policy decisions on tax and price incentives.

Although the CIA report is open to question because its conclusions are so sensitive to some doubtful numerical assumptions, its general proposition is meritorious, namely, that the world price of oil in the middle 1980s will be sensitive to current excess demands. Additional current excess demand originating in the Western Hemisphere may well be critically dependent upon public policy decisions on price and tax incentives for supply development. Of course, the extent of this demand will also depend upon how price and conservation policies affect consumption.

Nowhere is this more apt to be true than in the United States. As the world's largest consumer and producer of energy, the United States is notable because the net thrust of its energy policy is to discourage production and subsidize consumption. This is particularly true for oil and gas. This anomaly has already been an important factor in the price formation process in world oil markets, and it could again be important.

The following section discusses the potential for U.S. supply and the interrelationship between the oil and gas markets.

U.S. Supply and Demand
and Their Relation to the World Oil Market

The missing link in most discussions of world oil price prospects is the critical role played by the U.S. demand for imported oil. Specifically, such discussions rarely consider the interrelationships between (1) U.S. gas and oil markets and (2) the world oil market and the U.S. demand for imported oil.

The United States is the most significant factor on the demand side of the world oil market.[17] What is often overlooked is the relationship between domestic natural gas supply and the U.S. demand for imported oil. It should be obvious that a barrel of domestic oil production foregone is a barrel of foreign oil demanded.[18] What is equally important is that, on a Btu equivalent basis, a trillion cubic feet (tcf) of annual U.S. natural gas production is approximately equal to 500,000 barrels per day (b/d) of oil imports.[19]

The Relationship between the
World Oil and U.S. Natural Gas Markets

The minimum cost (before any security premium) of increased oil consumption to the U.S. economy is the world price of oil. The world price of oil is the OPEC price, and Saudi Arabia is clearly in a special position with respect to the OPEC price.

The interest of the United States is that increases in the price of world oil be smaller rather than larger. It is clear to us, at least, that the less pressure on Saudi capacity, the more the likelihood of smaller price increases.[20] One way to reduce such pressure is to maintain or increase U.S. natural gas supplies. Proponents of new gas deregulation argue that this would be the effect of such a policy.

Under deregulation of interstate natural gas markets, we believe the United States could increase natural gas production somewhat above current levels.[21] But even if deregulation only arrested or slowed the rate of decline of domestic production and additions to reserves, that would be significant in an opportunity sense. Keeping U.S. natural gas production higher than it would otherwise be is an addition to domestic energy supply.

The immediate replacement of any further declines in U.S. natural gas production will quite likely be with imported oil. Some replacement will be with synthetic natural gas (SNG) and liquefied natural gas (LNG) at substantially higher costs. The costs of direct SNG and LNG substitutes for regulation-induced shortages of natural gas are outlined in Table 1.5. There is also likely to be longer-run switching to electric heat pumps in some space heating markets. If the U.S. demand for imported oil were reduced by significantly greater domestic natural gas output than would otherwise be the case, the increase in pressure upon Saudi capacity would be substantially reduced.[22]

The Shadow Price of Natural Gas

How could raising the price of natural gas sold in the interstate market in the United States result in a lower U.S. demand for imported oil and hence less upward pressure upon the world price of oil? Since oil and gas are substitute fuels in many uses, would not an increase in the wellhead price of natural gas—which ultimately and inexorably would be reflected at the burner tip—result in an overall increase in the demand for oil?

We do not think so.

This is a supply and demand question. First, consider demand. Under regulation-induced shortage conditions, gas is not generally available as an alternative fuel at the controlled price. Increasingly, the job of regulation appears to be to allocate the shortages that regulation induces.

The relevant price of natural gas is the *shadow price* of gas at the shortage quantity. The shadow price of natural gas measures its social value; this value substantially exceeds the average transaction price in interstate markets.

Estimation of the effects of gas price increases on potential fuel switching is complicated by the existence in producing states of an unregulated, higher-price intrastate market alongside the regulated, lower-price interstate market.

TABLE 1.5

The Costs of Some Alternatives to
Conventional Natural Gas

Option	Btu/Standard Cubic Foot	Costs/ Btu	Date Costs Estimated	Lead Time
SNG from biomass (FPC certification of CRAP, Inc., Hooker, Oklahoma)	980	$1.33 plus up to $0.22 for transport	May 1976	2 years (for 3,500 Mcf/day)
Low Btu gas (from eastern coal at $24/ton; small scale)	125-165	$2.00 plus cleanup	Jan. 1977	1-2 years
Intermediate Btu gas (from eastern coal at $24/ton; large scale)	260-310	$1.90 plus cleanup	Jan. 1977	2-4 years
New LNG from Algeria to northeast U.S. (Tenneco)	1,018	$4.20	Dec. 1976 (projected for 1984)	8 years

SNG from propane, butane and natural gasoline	980	$4.25-$4.50	Jan. 1977	2 years
SNG from naphtha	980	$4.00-$5.00	Jan. 1977	2-1/3 years
SNG from western coal (El Paso)	954	$3.10	Mar. 1975	3 years
SNG from western coal (WESCO)	954	$4.50	Feb. 1977	5 years
Gas trapped in eastern coal beds	980	$1.44	Jan. 1977	5 years (for 150,000 Mcf/day)
Gas from Alaska (assuming well-head price of $1.70-$1.75)	1,018	$3.30-$3.90 depending on route	Jan. 1977 (projected for 1982-1983)	5 years

SOURCE:

Sources are FPC, Bureau of Mines, or private industry. Costs are set forth in dollars prospective for the year in which the project is to be completed. For purposes of comparison to alternative technologies, all capital subsidies (e.g., accelerated depreciation, investment tax credits) must be set forth explicitly.

FPC, National Gas Survey, Draft Final Report of the Transmission, Distribution and Storage Technical Advisory Task Force, Rate Design, May 1977, Chapter 6, p. 4.

A price-induced reallocation of supplies from the intrastate to the interstate market for natural gas would increase demand for oil to serve intrastate energy requirements; this increased demand, however, would be offset by reduced oil demand in the interstate market. The net effect is unclear, but we do not know of any econometric or other way to know a priori.

Nevertheless, continuing migration of industrial users of gas to producing states where natural gas is available at intrastate prices suggests that the shadow price of natural gas is substantially higher than the controlled price. Relative to oil, natural gas has superior convenience, flame quality, environment, and process input characteristics. Economic logic dictates that the current shadow price of natural gas at the regulation-induced shortage quantity is also higher than the market clearing price for natural gas under deregulation of natural gas markets.

The basic proposition is very simple. Deregulation of interstate natural gas markets and elimination of the regulation-induced shortage of natural gas would result in a decrease in the social shadow price of natural gas in determination of the overall supply and demand balance between gas and oil. In addition to the efficiency gains that would accrue from such a policy, the incremental U.S. demand for oil imports would be reduced, and the U.S. contribution to upward pressure on the OPEC price would be dampened.

Some Dimensions of the U.S. Natural Gas Market

Predicting oil or natural gas supply response to higher prices is a perilous exercise: recent conditions are far outside the range of our experience and are clouded by regulatory uncertainty. In addition, the discovery and development of new oil and gas reserves is a time-intensive and capital-intensive process, and even if prices had been free to reach market clearing levels, the adjustment process that began when the oil embargo radically altered price expectations would not yet be complete. The oil and gas resource base in the lower forty-eight states and contiguous offshore areas has in large part already been heavily explored, but higher prices—particularly in the intrastate natural gas markets—have allowed those markets to clear on both a production and additions-to-reserves basis.

The intrastate natural gas markets are of particular interest for several reasons. First, they indicate what Americans are willing to pay for energy. Second, the unregulated intrastate markets have been clearing on a competitive basis while the interstate natural gas market has been suffering regulation-induced shortages, which have contributed to (1) the U.S. demand for oil imports, and (2) upward pressure upon the world price of oil. And third, the Carter administration energy plan proposes to extend regulation to the intrastate markets and roll back the prices that have induced the supply additions that have permitted intrastate markets to clear. The Carter administration natural gas pricing proposals call for a wellhead price of $1.75 per thousand cubic feet (Mcf) for new gas supplies in the interstate and intrastate markets.

In recent years, prices in the intrastate natural gas markets have exceeded the ceiling prices in the interstate market. Most drilling and well completion decisions have been in response to intrastate market prices, and the prices in these markets have been responsible for most new supply additions in these years. The interstate market has been experiencing chronic shortages of production and reserves,[23] but intrastate markets have been clearing on both a production and additions-to-reserves basis.

As shown in Table 1.6, intrastate new supply first exceeded 50 percent of total new supply in 1970. In 1975, the response to intrastate market prices was such that the intrastate market was responsible for 87 percent of total new supply.

An increasingly significant fraction of new contract volumes in the intrastate markets has been sold at prices in the range of $2.01 to $2.50 per Mcf. In March 1977, 44.5

TABLE 1.6

Interstate Total Reserve Additions vs. Intrastate
Associated and Non-Associated Gas
(Excludes Alaska)

Year	AGA Reserve Additions Excluding Revisions (Tcf)	Interstate New Supply[1] Tcf	Interstate New Supply[1] Percent	Inferred Intrastate New Supply[2] Tcf	Inferred Intrastate New Supply[2] Percent
1966	14.8	10.0	68	4.8	32
1967	14.8	9.9	67	4.7	33
1968	9.8	6.4	65	3.4	35
1969	9.6	6.2	64	3.4	36
1970	11.3	3.5	31	7.8	69
1971	11.1	2.2	20	8.9	80
1972	10.7	5.0	47	5.7	53
1973	10.1	1.7	17	8.4	83
1974	9.7	2.4	25	7.3	75
1975	10.0	1.3[3]	13	8.7	87

SOURCE:

Federal Power Commission, Opinion 770-A, Docket No. RM 75-14, p. 116.

(1) Form 15, FPC, excluding revisions.

(2) Derived by assuming that intrastate reserve additions are equal to the difference between total AGA reserve additions and the reserve additions committed to the interstate market.

(3) Preliminary.

percent of all new intrastate contract volumes received $2.01 to $2.50 per Mcf; for the January-March quarter itself, the fraction was 28.7 percent. In the January-March quarter of 1977, Texas accounted for 59 percent of all new intrastate contract volumes, and 33 percent of new Texas intrastate suppliers were priced in the $2.01 to $2.50 range.

The Carter administration natural gas pricing proposals involve the extension of ceiling price regulation and vintaging to the intrastate markets. We believe that the price rollback in the intrastate markets will (1) aggravate the regulation-induced natural gas shortage, and (2) increase the U.S. demand for imported oil.

In addition, the Carter administration oil pricing proposals, which create an additional category of "new-new" oil, further elaborate the "vintaging" concept for oil. The vintaging concept—an attempt to use the authority of the state to monopsonize the domestic supplies of oil and gas—has been tested in practice in the interstate natural gas market by the Federal Power Commission (FPC). Its legacy is the regulation-induced shortage of natural gas. The vintaging concept appears headed for still wider application,[24] and its basic effects upon supply response are therefore of considerable interest.

If prices are based upon a vintaging system, the effect is to truncate the probability distribution of expected returns. Even if later economic conditions warrant it, prices for the oil and gas that may be discovered by wells commenced in a particular vintage period cannot exceed the ceiling price established for that vintage. As a result, a vintaging system must inhibit supply response in a period when prices are expected to rise. In addition, if there are substantial lags in the actual process of establishing vintage prices or if the vintaging system increases price uncertainty as a result of rollback or administrative discretion, the supply inhibition is worsened. The chronic shortages of reserves and production in the interstate gas market have been a result of both the fact that the vintage ceiling prices have been too low and the effect and operation of the vintaging system itself.[25]

If the vintaging system in domestic oil and natural gas production is extended, domestic supply response will probably continue to be inhibited.

Potential Domestic Supply Response

The potential domestic supply response is a function of the domestic resource base; the rate and conditions under which companies have access to the resource base in the

TABLE 1.7
The Range of Potential 1985
U.S. Supply Response

Source	mmb/d
Known fields (including enhanced oil recovery)	3 - 5
Alaska (including NPR-4)	1 - 3
New Onshore and Offshore Production (including Atlantic OCS and deep Gulf of Mexico)	1 - 4
Incremental Natural Gas Equivalent	0 - 3
TOTAL	5 -15

SOURCE:

Authors' estimates.

Outer Continental Shelf (OCS), in the federal domain, and in frontier Alaskan areas; tax policies; the price profile; and the way industry perceives the expected price profile and price formation process. These economic/regulatory and geologic factors combine to produce a range of prospective supply response.

In our judgment, the components of such a range may break down as illustrated in Table 1.7. The high end of the range, of course, is based upon assumptions that the prices for at least new domestic oil and natural gas are free to equate with world levels, that the current tax treatment of income from oil and gas production is unchanged,[26] and that optimistic assumptions hold with respect to the resource base[27] and industry access to that resource base.

Because there is so much uncertainty about all these factors, it is impossible precisely to attribute components of the range to the individual factors that contribute to it. But if one arbitrarily divides the 10 mmb/d range evenly between economic/regulatory and geological factors, the half (5 mmb/d) attributable to economic/regulatory effects exceeds the 3.5-4.5 mmb/d 1985 Soviet world demand for OPEC oil projected by the CIA.

In a recent publication, the Federal Energy Administration (FEA) forecast production 2 mmb/d higher than that forecast for 1985 by the ICA,[28] in the absence of post-1979 crude oil price controls. Although opinions vary about the long-term response of domestic crude supply to price, a *potential* 20 percent increase in domestic production relative to a base assuming price controls, continued delay in OCS leasing, and substantial regulatory disincentives for exploration do not seem unreasonable by 1985. Moreover, the differential could be considerably larger. In our opinion, the U.S. economic and regulatory policies that affect domestic oil and gas supply are apt to have a larger effect upon world oil prices in 1985 than the potential Soviet import demand will have.

The Sensitivity of National Security Considerations to Alternative World Supply Developments

Modification of the CIA Forecast

If the CIA forecast in Table 1.3 is modified in accordance with the assumptions discussed above—that 1985 Soviet/Eastern bloc oil supply and demand are roughly in balance, that Western Hemisphere supply in 1985 is 2 mmb/d higher than the CIA forecast, and that U.S. supply in 1985 is 20 percent higher than the CIA forecast—the CIA conclusions are modified as follows.

First, OPEC production needs in 1985 decline to 38-43 mmb/d. If OPEC productive capacity (excluding Saudi Arabia) remains at 27-29 mmb/d in 1985, as forecast by the CIA, required Saudi Arabian output will be limited to about 12 mmb/d per day, well within the physical capacity projected even for 1980 and not substantially higher than present peak production. Under these assumptions, it is less likely that a substantial constant dollar price increase will occur.

Just as significantly, the United States still would be importing nearly 50 percent of its total oil needs, but as much as half of its imports could be from Western Hemisphere sources. More probably, as much as half would be from non-Persian Gulf sources. The national security aspects of our energy policy in 1985 would be different from those we now face. In addition, Europe and Japan would be substantially more dependent on Persian Gulf producers—and on the Soviet Union—than the United States would be, thereby posing possible major divergences of views among OECD members. (To the extent that Western Europe would also depend heavily on U.S. coal, the divergence of views could be magnified.)

Political Issues That Will
Influence the World Oil Market

Herman Kahn has noted that our major social problems over the next two centuries are not tied to the existence of raw materials.[29] They depend on the ability of our institutions, particularly governmental ones, to meet social needs equitably and at least cost.

Even over the next ten to twenty-five years, changes in government policy can have a major effect on the supply, demand, and price of oil and gas. In addition to the prior discussion of the effect of U.S. policy on price and supply of natural gas, certain of the important policy issues are noted below, in diminishing order of importance, although not in order of probability.

First, Saudi Arabia can choose—for a variety of reasons, whether or not linked to Middle East or internal politics, threats from Iran, negotiations with Israel, or internal philosophical premises—to reduce production to a minimum level to meet internal revenue needs, say 6 mmb/d. In the foreseeable future, such a decision would lead inevitably to a tremendous increase in oil prices, with world economic disruption as countries and economies adjusted to higher prices, scarcities, etc.[30] Predictably, the losers in such an action would be, first, Third World countries with no other source of oil; then Japan, with no indigenous supply of oil; then Western Europe; and last, the United States. (The pattern reflects relative degrees of "self-sufficiency.") To what extent the instability caused by such an action would be followed by other destabilizing actions, including military ones, is difficult to predict. But we underline the importance over the next five to ten years of the assumption concerning Saudi Arabia's production.

Second, a major barrier to increased production from new areas at present is the political risk that oil companies face as they negotiate contractual exploration and production arrangements in these new areas. Historically, governments have extensively taxed production from successful drilling efforts, even though the returns from such efforts must permit recovery of the costs of concomitant failures. As a result, taxing on a political basis, rather than on the basis of real resource cost, will presumably lead to the production of less oil than would otherwise have been the case and hence to higher prices for current output. There is an important need for international mechanisms that spread both the risk and the returns from exploration and production across national boundaries for the producing countries' accounts (particularly Third World countries). Recent internal World Bank discussions have addressed this problem, and apparently the World Bank itself is prepared to perform some of the portion of the risk-sharing function.[31]

We think that it is significant and disappointing that the Carter energy plan makes no attempt to deal with the development of new conventional sources outside of the United States, particularly with respect to proposed risk-sharing mechanisms. We feel that such a mechanism would be extremely valuable in a variety of contexts (e.g., U.S.-Third World relations) and could lead to cheaper and more secure energy, relative to the premium prices we face for energy from

LNG, coal liquefaction or gasification, and even oil shale.

A third political issue is the potential for regulated scarcity of low-sulfur crude and fuel oil. In Los Angeles, for example, the sulfur standards for utility fuel oil recently have been reduced from 0.5 percent sulfur to 0.25 percent sulfur, the cost of which will be borne in part by all U.S. gasoline and heating oil customers through the current "entitlements" program.[32] Certain Western European governments are apparently considering lowering sulfur standards in response to relatively greater availability of North Sea low-sulfur crude oil. Were the Japanese to lower their sulfur standards as well, both the competition for low-sulfur crude oil and the long-run price of low-sulfur products (obtained in part through increasingly expensive desulfurization processes) would increase dramatically.

Finally, there is a developing nationalistic impulse to refine and market products in the same countries that produce the crude oils. Continued capitulation to this impulse on any significant scale could add measurably to consumer cost. Two prime examples involve the disposal of Alaskan crude oil and UK North Sea crude oil. The former is to be used in retrofitted West Coast refineries or in Midwest refineries—only after a long ocean voyage in relatively small tankers, or only after construction of trans–United States pipelines—as opposed to simple exchanges with Japan for Middle East oil. Similarly the British government intends to refine up to two-thirds of its North Sea production in the United Kingdom—despite projected enormous expense for refinery construction and retrofit, and the availability of substantially underutilized refining capacity in other parts of Western Europe.

The Energy Crisis Revisited

As noted above, the energy "crisis" has two aspects: the first is the transition within the United States to higher relative prices of energy; the second is a long-term readjustment of the world economies to differing degrees of energy self-sufficiency and different intercountry energy trade patterns than now exist. But we do not think the "crisis" involves "running out" in the near term, and if political institutions behave sensibly, it may not involve another significant price increase in the mid-1980s.

The appropriate short-term price adjustment policy is related to issues of tax policy, income redistribution, and regional economic development. The acrimonious debate that has continued now for several months over the Carter energy proposals indicates an extraordinary lack of consensus on the appropriate transitional mechanisms and expresses the basic human conflicts between "haves" and "have nots."

Economists concerned about the efficiency of resource allocation prefer to see the quickest possible adjustment to prices established by willing buyers and willing sellers in a market in which prices equal replacement costs of marginal units. But the political constraints that impede this adjustment are severe. We do not propose a new price-adjustment mechanism, but rather note (1) that the conclusions reached earlier are sensitive to the price-adjustment mechanisms that the U.S. government proposes, and (2) that sensitivity involves spillovers into the world oil market.

Currently proposed policies appear likely to reduce U.S. supply and increase U.S. demand over what would otherwise occur—either under a continuation of the regulatory status quo or under a significant initiative to decontrol and deregulate U.S. oil and gas markets. Furthermore, the apparent savings to consumers from continued price controls are apt to be illusory. The incremental fuel continues to be high-cost imported oil, and the cost of that oil may increase substantially over the next ten years if some of the political variables discussed earlier turn negative. On the demand side of the balance, the United States is a significant factor in the price formation process in the world oil market. Continued deterioration of the internal U.S. oil and gas supply and demand balance could be a considerably greater force in the price formation environment of the 1980s than the Soviets' import demands will be.

We also are concerned about the long-run aspect of the energy crisis, in which the United States develops its oil, gas, and, particularly, coal resources to the extent that its dependence on others diminishes dramatically by the mid-1980s. Europe and Japan, particularly, and much of the Third World will continue to be dependent on OPEC oil production for energy to fuel economic growth. The world could conceivably develop into a bimodal energy system in which the United States is the balance wheel in the international coal market, and Saudi Arabia continues to be the balance wheel for oil. Simultaneously, Western Europe will probably be more dependent on Soviet oil and gas. These trends will have uncertain, but important, political consequences for the industrial trading world in general and for the United States in particular.

Conclusions

We conclude that the energy crisis is indeed less one of raw materials than one of money, which trades off with national security. If we want to achieve significant reductions in imports, the "moral equivalent of war" will not be enough. Stronger measures will be required. Such stronger measures may include increased authoritarian intervention with regard to what U.S. energy consumers can, cannot, and must do. But national security may be as well, or better, enhanced in other ways at less long-term economic, political, and social cost. Since imports are the difference between domestic supply and demand, a substitute for mandated reduction of U.S. energy demands is more development of higher-cost domestic oil and gas production from conventional, but previously undeveloped, sources.

In our view, the current policies of the Carter administration—particularly the perverse incentives for supply creation and reliance on governmental regulation and standards to replace individual investment decisions—could easily lead to higher prices and less certain supply.

Notes

1. It is important as an aside to examine briefly the role of supply and demand in a market context. The market mechanism is a means for achieving an efficient allocation of resources. Markets, when they are allowed to operate, perform a continuous and decentralized benefit-cost analysis. Supply reflects costs. Demand reflects benefits. Decisions with regard to increased consumption and production are made on the basis of current and expected prices according to the many special details that affect particular situations. These decisions are made by those in the best position to evaluate the benefits and costs to themselves: individual consumers and producers. Regulation, controls, and administrative decision making can never duplicate the pattern of results that market action achieves, or the flexibility with which markets adjust to changed circumstances.

When a market is clearing at a given price, it has adjusted to changed circumstances and supply equals demand. The fundamental changed circumstance in world energy markets has been the dramatic increase in the price of oil. The form of energy with which Americans are most familiar is gasoline. It is instructive to use gasoline as an example and to consider what sort of incentive prices suppliers would face, in the absence of regulation, at gasoline prices that are not beyond the bounds of reasonable consideration. We arbitrarily use one dollar per gallon for illustrative purposes. Under current taxes, refinery margins, and distribution costs, it would take crude oil prices—across the board for old, new, stripper, imported, etc., oil—on the order of $25-$30 per barrel to cause gasoline prices to be in the neighborhood of one dollar per gallon. Current weighted average U.S. refinery input costs are about $12 per barrel and weighted average U.S. crude oil prices are $8.40 per barrel.

The magnitudes of the U.S. and world supply responses at crude oil prices consistent with U.S. gasoline prices of one dollar per gallon are unknown. But an intuitive estimate is that such prices would postpone for an indefinite period the problem of "running out" of energy, even oil and gas. Whether such prices are in the immediate offing is the problem we further address below.

2. *Harper's,* July 1977, pp. 7-9. This paper was in final draft form before the appearance of Lapham's "The Energy Debacle," *Harper's,* August 1977, pp. 58-74. As the reader will see below, we are in basic sympathy with Lapham's perspective.

3. See, for example, *National Journal,* July 2, 1977, p. 1050, for a discussion of recent public opinion polls on energy issues.

4. U.S., Central Intelligence Agency, Memorandum ER77-102YOU; McLean, Virginia, April 1977.

5. There is a movement by forecasters to project long-run shifts from oil and gas to coal, nuclear power, shale, solar power, hydro-power, and other sources of energy. These models—including the Gulf Oil/SRI model, those developed by Nordhaus, and others—attempt to forecast supply and demand through the year 2100 or some relatively distant period. At the risk of appearing shortsighted, we are willing to overlook for present purposes the crises predicted even in the first quarter of the twenty-first century.

6. CIA, Memorandum ER77-102YOU, p. 15.

7. Cabinet Task Force on Oil Import Control, *The Oil Import Question* (Washington, D.C.: Government Printing Office, 1970). The authors participated in the preparation of this report.

8. The reference price used by the Cabinet Task Force for U.S. oil supply was $3.30 per barrel. When $5.25 per barrel in 1977 dollars (the upper limit for old oil) is adjusted for inflation and the loss of percentage depletion, the economic incentive to maintain production in existing U.S. fields turns out to be equivalent to approximately $2.50 per barrel in 1969-1970 dollars. This 25 percent decline in incentives is responsible, we believe, for a significant portion of the decline in oil output from established U.S. oil fields. The adjustment for inflation uses the wholesale price index. The adjustment for the loss of depletion further reduces economic incentives by approximately 14 percent.

9. For completeness, it is important to note that Canadian production was estimated in 1969 to be as high as 4 million barrels per day by 1980, but is now projected to be substantially below that. Venezuelan production, in addition, was expected to be somewhat higher than it now is. On the other hand, in 1969, no production was assumed from either North Sea or Mexican reserves, which together by 1980 could yield as much as 5-7 mmb/d, according to the CIA forecast.

10. See, for example, Edward W. Erickson and Herbert S. Wino-kur, "Companies, Nations and Markets: Multinational Corporations and International Oil," forthcoming, Fraser Institute, Vancouver, British Columbia. The analysis upon which this article is based, and the article itself, were completed in the spring and summer of 1976.

11. The forecasts seem reasonable to us, compared to others we have seen. At least one major consulting firm forecasts much lower demand. But the potential for conservation, either to reduce demand or when considered as new "supply," is still poorly understood, and continued savings will be difficult and expensive to achieve over a ten-year period.

12. These claims and some analysis of their validity are well discussed in several sources. One quoted extensively here is a series of articles in *Total Information,* no. 68, 1976. Others include Jeremy Russell, *Energy as a Factor in Soviet Energy Policy* (Lexington, Mass.: Saxon House/Lexington Books, 1976); and the U.S., Congress, Library of Congress, Congressional Research Service, "Project Interdependence: U.S. and World Energy Outlook through 1990," June 1977.

13. *Total Information,* no. 68, 1976, p. 6. Russell, *Soviet Energy Policy,* notes that "the main problem here is not that the Soviet Union is short of energy resources but that it is not able to make a good use of those which it has" (p. 34) and that "it is probably fair to say that, from the Soviet point of view, things are not as bad as they appear to be to Western observers, although there is clearly a great deal of room for improvement" (p. 35).

14. Xavier Boy de la Tour, "Oil in the U.S.S.R.," *Total Information,* no. 68, 1976, p. 9. Even if these cost figures are subject to the same expansion factors that have plagued U.S. oil shale, Canadian and Venezuelan heavy oil, and the Alaska pipeline, they suggest that a substantial further world oil price increase will be a result of marketing strategies and the price required to call forth considerable additional supply, rather than a "skittering off the edge of the cliff" into an abyss where no additional supply is available at any price.

15. *Total Information,* no. 68, 1976, p. 6.

16. Platt's *Oilgram,* June 17, 1977, p. 5.

17. In recent years, the U.S. demand for imported oil has been approximately equal to total Saudi Arabian output. In the winter of 1977, when the U.S. demand for imported oil jumped from about 7 million barrels per day to about 10 million barrels per day, that incremental 3 million barrels per day was *greater* than the total output of *any* of the following countries or areas: Iraq, Kuwait, Abu Dhabi, Libya, Algeria, Nigeria, Venezuela, Indonesia, Canada, Prudhoe Bay, or the North Sea. In terms of that portion of world oil supply that moves directly in international commerce, the incremental U.S. demand for imported oil that occurred in the winter of 1977 was greater than the output of any single country in the world with the exceptions of Iran and Saudi Arabia. In terms of world oil supply primarily consumed in

the countries in which it is produced, only the production of the United States and of the USSR has in recent years exceeded the total U.S. demand for imports—and if current trends persist, the United States itself may shortly be importing more than half its oil requirements on a regular basis. During the winter of 1977, imports briefly accounted for over 50 percent of total U.S. demand.

18. This somewhat oversimplifies the case. U.S. crude oil production—even "new-new" oil—is price-controlled at levels below the landed price of foreign crude. Therefore, an incremental barrel of foreign crude oil raises the weighted average U.S. product price by more than an incremental barrel of U.S. production. Under these conditions, and with a negative elasticity of demand, a barrel of U.S. oil production foregone results in somewhat less than a barrel of foreign oil demanded.

19. But this issue is at most secondary. Peak U.S. natural gas production approximated 23 tcf per year. In the last several years, U.S. natural gas production has declined to about 19 tcf per year. The loss of 4 tcf per year is equivalent to almost 2 million barrels per day of oil imports. This is greater than the oil output of any one of over three dozen countries, including Canada, the United Kingdom, Norway, Abu Dhabi, Kuwait, Indonesia, Algeria, Mexico, Australia, China, Ecuador, Dubai, Qatar, Brunei-Malaysia, and Romania.

As a result of crude and product price controls in the United States, we sell refined products at lower prices than those consistent with world oil prices. This means that the goods and services we export to pay for oil imports are more valuable in terms of consumer welfare foregone than the increase in welfare associated with incremental oil consumption. This export drain is a net efficiency loss to the economy, but that is another story.

20. Throughout the following, price references will be to nominal prices. Capacity estimates are always economically suspect, particularly if they refer to output rates beyond the range of experience. There is little reason to believe Saudi capacity numbers are any different. Suffice it to repeat the truism that, other things equal, the higher the rate of Saudi output, the higher the rate of Saudi capacity utilization.

21. This optimism, of course, is contingent upon timely access to OCS areas.

22. There are large economic benefits, too. At current levels of imports, improving the U.S. internal supply and demand balance for energy would only have to restrain the OPEC price by a dollar per barrel in order for it to generate about $3.1 billion per year in payoff for *all* U.S. energy users. At higher levels of imports, the payoff to U.S. energy users is correspondingly greater.

This is, however, a partial calculation. U.S. natural gas producers are American firms and citizens. Thus, higher natural gas prices, which are a cost to U.S. energy users, are a revenue for U.S. natural gas producers and are subject to U.S. tax policy. On a national basis, any restraint on OPEC prices that is a result of deregulating U.S. natural gas markets would be a complete social benefit.

There is another benefit as well. If deregulating interstate natural gas prices results in a U.S. energy supply and demand balance that reduces the U.S. demand for imported oil by 1 mmb/d from what it would otherwise have been, this opportunity saving may be approximated as an increase in U.S. national income at the full price of imported oil. At current landed prices of $14-$16 per barrel, this amounts to over $5.0 billion per year. This amount alone could justify new natural gas price deregulation on an incremental, national benefit-cost calculation.

Thus, improvements in the efficiency of resource allocation in the U.S. economy have a double benefit. The first benefit is the efficiency gain itself. The second is the expected value of any savings in terms of transfers to OPEC.

23. In 1976, net curtailments of 3.2 tcf exceeded 25 percent of the approximately 12 tcf of natural gas moving in the interstate market.

24. The thought here is with particular reference to additional vintages for oil and gas. But if the U.S. supply of coal is less than perfectly elastic, increasing reliance upon coal will result in economic rents for inframarginal units. In this case, we might expect extension of price controls and vintaging to the coal market.

25. In the intrastate markets, higher prices, the absence of a vintaging system, the relatively short terms of many contracts, and provisions that allow contract renegotiation and amendments have together allowed the full probability distribution of future expected returns to affect current investment decisions to risk funds to attempt to create new natural gas additions. It is the operation of this process that has allowed the intrastate market to clear on both a production and additions-to-reserves basis.

26. For a discussion of the effects of tax policy, see E. W. Erickson, S. W. Millsaps, and R. M. Spann, "Oil Supply and Tax Incentives," *Brookings Papers on Economic Activity* 2(1974): 449-478.

27. See, for example, National Petroleum Council, *Enhanced Oil Recovery* (Washington: NPC, 1976).

28. FEA Draft *1977 National Energy Outlook,* January 15, 1977. Executive Summary, p. 14. This forecast assumes that real world oil prices increase at 2 percent per annum and phaseout of current price regulations.

29. Herman Kahn, William Brown, and Leon Martel, *The Next 200 Years* (New York: William Morrow & Co., 1976).

30. In terms of how the world oil market has worked, a decrease in Saudi output would be achieved by an increase in the Saudi tax rate, and hence the tax-paid Saudi price. Other countries would then increase their tax rates, companies would realign liftings, and the decrease in Saudi output would follow from their role as supplier of last resort. Output changes would be initiated by price changes, but the price changes would be conditioned upon a decision to reduce output. For this reason, we discuss an output decision in the text. See Erickson and Winokur, "Companies, Nations and Markets."

31. For a public discussion of risk-sharing plans now being considered by the World Bank and the Overseas Private Investment Corporation, see *Business Week,* July 18, 1977, pp. 18-19.

32. Production of lower-sulfur-content fuel oil requires a greater proportion of imported low-sulfur crude oil, the cost of which is subsidized by payments from refiners using a high proportion of "old" domestic oil. To some extent, the higher crude costs of these latter refiners are passed along to consumers of the finished products.

2
Energy Scarcity and the U.S. Economic Future

James W. McKie

The energy crisis is the epiphany of the 1970s.[1] It has many troublesome aspects, but I propose to concentrate on only one: the economic consequences for the United States in the moderately long run, by which I mean the next fifty years or so. Does the end of cheap energy mean the end of economic growth? Can even the present levels of U.S. output and employment be sustained as energy becomes scarcer and costlier?

For well over a hundred years, the accelerating pace of economic growth in the world has been accompanied by a similar acceleration in the use of energy—in the application of energy-based technology to produce more output with less input and in the substitution of energy for raw human and animal labor power.

In the United States, to consider only the present century, energy consumption by industry and by final consumers grew at a rate of 3.2 percent per year up to 1970, and the real gross national product (GNP) grew at a slightly higher rate, 3.3 percent.[2] Though energy consumption per capita has not been perfectly correlated with real income per capita, there has been a strong tendency for higher GNP to involve higher use of energy. Similar correlations (though with different coefficients) can be observed elsewhere in the world. These relationships have led many observers to conclude that high real income, self-sustaining growth, and full or nearly full employment *depend* on the availability of cheap and abundant energy, such as the world has had available to it during the last 100 years and more.

The long secular decline in real energy prices was one of the reasons for the lavish use of energy that developed over that period. Energy was cheap; it was becoming cheaper; it was available in seemingly unlimited amounts to the industrialized economies. Not surprisingly, we in the United States used a lot of it. We did not think of energy resources as a factor *limiting* growth, but as a factor *stimulating* growth. When we look back on that period, which ended only about six years ago, it is quite apparent that most of our plans, forecasts, technological systems, developmental blueprints, and even our science fiction simply assumed that unlimited quantities of energy would be available at low cost to support any system, any technology, any design, any gadget we chose to put into operation. Even the resource problems that we had begun to worry about—mostly involving minerals or forest products—could be solved with high-energy technology calling upon a highly elastic supply.

The Return of Malthus

The essentially boundless view of economic growth so characteristic of the middle twentieth century has not always been the dominant view in economics. A hundred and fifty years ago, the theme was gloomy. In the view of that time, economic systems could grow as capital investment accumulated and as the labor force increased along with population. Incomes could increase for a time. But there was an inescapable brake on the process: the limited supply of natural resources, especially land. The most famous of these formulations was that of T. R. Malthus. In his world, population would grow, but the food supply would not grow in proportion. Real wages would decline to a minimum subsistence level; profits would fall to zero, and capital investment would eventually cease; life would become more and more miserable until finally population growth stopped. The economic system would have reached a stationary state. That was the inevitable goal of growth. These predictions were what earned economics the name of "the dismal science."

In the view of growth that later became dominant, the constraints imposed by limited endowments of natural resources and energy had dropped out of the picture. What eased these constraints was a factor ignored by Malthus—technological change. The new view was that better techniques of production could outweigh any resource scarcity by making the existing resources more productive and by developing new resources. Productivity could grow faster than population. Population itself would not increase at a rate determined simply by the food supply. Let us call this the "steady-growth" or "balanced-growth" school. As it was finally perfected in the 1950s, the steady-growth theory held that growth depended only on labor and investment—the reproducible capital stock—plus the influence of constant accretions to technological knowledge.[3] There were no physical limits to expansion of the means of production. Per capita income need not fall; it could grow without limit. The economy need not approach stasis. This approach to growth, of course, fitted the observed facts, at least in the Western world, better than the Malthusian predictions did, so it is not surprising that those predictions were pretty much forgotten for a long time except by those who had direct experiences with places such as Bangladesh.

We all know what has happened since 1970: Dr. Malthus has returned in a new incarnation, armed with the computer and with a vastly more elaborate vision of the disaster that is bound to overtake us.[4] No longer is it a simple result of the pressure of population on the food supply, but a combination of population and economic growth pressing on all types of limited or exhaustible resources. The stationary state—in a form of "world collapse" even more dire than that foreseen by the early Malthusians—has reappeared in the future, evidently no later than the middle of the twenty-first century.

We will not stop to describe the findings of the Club of Rome or the many attacks upon them. Nor will we catalog the developing literature of the no-growth school.[5] This literature is in large part a reaction by environmentalists to what they perceive as the consequences of economic growth, but it includes more than concern for the physical environment. The sudden swing in philosophical outlook has resulted from the events that have crowded in upon us so fast since 1970—the food crisis, the environmental crisis, the energy crisis and the emerging threats of depletion of other resources on which the world economy now depends, the population crisis, the confrontation between rich and poor nations, between developed economies and those supplying raw materials. It is no wonder that the predictions of an early halt to economic growth have so readily found supporters.

Depletable Resources and Economic Growth

Although the prophets of steady growth usually assumed that energy resources would continue to be cheap and abundant and hence required no special attention as elements in economic growth, their models were certainly capable of incorporating any changes in natural resource availability. They simply assumed that reproducible capital was a very good substitute for depletable resources and that where it was not, technological change would overcome the scarcity.[6]

In this standard economic theory, the price system (given the right conditions) can conserve *any* exhaustible resource so as to give the best possible uses over time. When any depletable resource—such as a form of energy—begins to show signs of "running out," a market-oriented economy should put out increasingly strong signals that this is happening. This should take the form of higher prices—provided, of course, that people (and governments) read the future correctly and provided that no one is manipulating the price to achieve purposes other than economical use of the resource over time. The fact that real prices for energy did *not* rise steadily during the period 1920-1970 simply meant that future scarcities were not manifesting themselves in forms that people (or governments, whose foresight is usually no better) could easily discern. Technological progress was improving the efficiency of energy use, and new sources were being developed sufficiently rapidly to offset depletion even while real energy prices were declining. But by the early 1970s, all that had apparently changed.

In trying to discern what will happen in the future, we are very much the victims of present circumstances and present information. We have recently seen how rapidly those can change, so that the same future looks very different from year to year. But let us assume that the pessimistic projections of the 1970s are correct and that supplies of conventional hydrocarbon fuels in the world are being rapidly depleted without much prospect of renewal by discovery of now unknown reserves—in other words, that the world will actually follow a King Hubbert depletion curve on oil and gas into the next century.[7] Let us also assume that costs of alternatives (including environmental costs) are a good deal higher than historic prices of oil and gas and that the technologies of some potential substitutes will be slow to develop.

Put this way, the problem of energy sounds somewhat less threatening than in the scenario of supplies vanishing as an energy-hungry world sinks into famine and disintegration. Yet the depletion of supplies of conventional hydrocarbons as energy costs and prices go on rising does threaten to restrain economic growth. Not only must we use less energy than we would have used if energy had remained cheap. In addition, more and more of society's resources must go into providing us with the energy we do use—resources that could otherwise have provided other valuable goods and services.

This problem was not seen to exist until recently. How will the economy of the United States, specifically, react to rising real cost of energy? That is the best way to formulate the *economic* problem of energy, though not, of course, the political problems.

Reactions to Higher Energy Prices

In general, economists believe that a complete answer to the problem of higher energy prices should make use of four properties of our economic system that are often overlooked.

The first is that energy is itself a produced good, not an absolutely fixed stock. Its availability to the economy depends on its price, through the process of investment in the energy industries. The economy tends to react to a developing energy "scarcity" by devoting more of its other resources —capital and labor—to production of energy, if normal economic incentives are allowed to do their usual work. The augmentation of energy output then depends on costs and prices —in economists' jargon, on the elasticity of supply. Of course, the picture is complicated when some of the supply is imported and its price is under the control of foreign monopolists.

The second is that energy is an *input* to the production process; in most applications, nonenergy inputs can to some degree be substituted for energy. How much so depends again on relative price changes. We have used energy-intensive processes in the past partly because energy was so cheap relative to other factors of production, not because we had to produce goods and services in exactly that way.

The third is that goods and services are substitutes for each other, and they do not use the same amount of energy even when they serve much the same purposes. As energy (or a particular kind of energy, such as oil) becomes more expensive, the goods and services embodying it will become relatively more costly, and consumers will shift their purchases toward substitutes that embody less. These effects may be as great or greater than the direct reduction of energy consumption caused by higher real prices. Moreover, the substitution effect becomes stronger with the passage of time.

(The fourth property of the system we shall consider in a moment.)

These two substitution effects—of inputs and of outputs —in a flexible, complex economic structure are bound to be widespread and pervasive. We can expect, for example, that higher energy prices in the future will have some effects on the way we design and lay out cities—not only through government policy toward zoning and mass transit but also through the effect of price signals on consumer behavior. The economic value of living nearer to the central city and of locating workplaces near transportation nodes may at last reverse the trend toward suburban sprawl that has been the American way of life for thirty years or more. I must admit that these changes of direction would be particularly difficult, and few signs of them are visible yet.

We are probably on the threshold of a change in building design: the glass ziggurat, which has become so familiar in the Western world since 1945, and which requires huge infusions of energy to be habitable at all even on the balmiest days, may be on the way out. Similarly, domestic home design is beginning to give considerable weight to insulation and heat exchange as substitutes for fuel, thus reinforcing the direct price effects that may lead consumers to stop overheating their houses in winter and to get used to being somewhat warmer in the summer.

Food production in the United States has become highly energy-intensive for running farm machinery, drying crops, packaging, and distributing over long distances. One authority has estimated that we consume ten calories of energy in the United States to produce every calorie of food on the consumer's table.[8] Technological change in the future will probably be directed to energy-saving rather than energy-

using techniques, even if they involve using more labor per
unit of output. Even the "green revolution" in other parts of
the world will no longer expand on the implicit assumption
that cheap energy could make fertilizer and other agricultural
inputs available without limit at low cost.

Examples both important and trivial can be multiplied
endlessly. One would expect the aluminum beer can to become more expensive to use than the tinplated steel one, and
that in turn more costly than the returnable bottle; we may
be back to a keg on every hearth before we know it. A recent
study for the Senate Interior Committee found that the
energy "ratios" for container systems were roughly as
follows, for one gallon of beer in twelve-ounce containers:[9]

		Ratio to Returnable Bottles
Aluminum cans	69,000 Btu	3.9
Steel cans, aluminum tops	51,800 Btu	2.9
Disposable bottles	44,500 Btu	2.5
Returnable bottles	17,800 Btu	1.0

Thus, we can save about three-fourths of the energy in an
all-aluminum beer can "system" by reverting to returnable
bottles. Or even more, perhaps, by reverting to kegs, bung
starters, and pitchers.

Vacationers confronted with high fuel costs may not only
drive smaller and lighter automobiles but also leave them in
one spot while camping and hiking instead of taking the
cross-country tour of seven national monuments in seven
days seen from the car window only. Local consumer goods
industries may gain at the expense, say, of bread and ice
cream trucked in from the distant metropolis. All this may
happen in response to energy prices, in addition to any effect
that a national conservation campaign may have.

Nor will these changes necessarily be retrogressions to an
earlier way of life—even the beer keg may be made of a wood
substitute. As noted above, scarcities will direct future

changes in energy technology toward the development of substitute processes and inputs, toward innovations that economize energy, such as miniaturization. Technology will be instrumental chiefly in developing new forms of energy to take the place of diminishing conventional supplies. So this is the fourth property of a complex industrialized economy that we must bear in mind in assessing the influence of energy resource depletion on economic growth: technology is not blind. Technological advance in large part responds to developing needs, and energy prices are now signaling rather pressing needs to "economize" both demand and supply.

Economic Predictions: Energy Prices and Growth

The Backstop

Future energy prices, inputs, and outputs depend on an exceedingly complex process of relative growth and substitution. Unfortunately, estimates of some crucial parts of that mechanism are uncertain. For example, the development of alternative energy sources is hard to estimate very far into the future. But most "models" of the process used by economists, engineers, and systems analysts assume that there will be a "backstop"—or two or three—to rescue us from the depletion of prime energy sources, which are now running out, chiefly conventional hydrocarbons.

By "backstop" we mean that more abundant supplies of energy in some form will become available at a later date and at a higher real cost than the historical costs of the now favored modes, which are more limited in amount.[10] If there is a backstop, then energy conservation at present, and energy prices in the near future, become a matter of making a successful transition to dependence on the backstop source at higher prices. If there is no backstop, then the present energy economy becomes a closed system, and all we can do is make supplies last as long as we can while real prices of resources rise exponentially without limit.

Historically, of course, we have moved from one type of energy to another along a series of *falling* cost levels. The various types have for the most part continued in use side by side while finding their spheres of relative advantage. But the backstop assumption is that real costs will shift upward as conventional oil and gas are essentially phased out and that real energy prices must shift upward with them.

Several energy backstops appear possible for the U.S. economy over intervals of the receding future. The first is coal, assuming that the technologies of coal gasification and coal liquefaction will be developed as the switch to a coal-based energy economy is occurring. The second—farther along—is nuclear, assuming again that the technology of production and disposition for the breeder reactor (or, eventually, the technology of the fusion reactor) is perfected in the meantime. The third is solar, which may never materialize as an economic source. We do not know what the cost thresholds for coal-based energy and nuclear energy based on U-238 will be, but it is usually assumed that the supply will be quite elastic once those thresholds are reached. The depletion scale for coal is much longer than for oil and gas, though as with petroleum its costs of development may increase over time unless offset by advances in technology. If nuclear power can safely be made self-generating, there will no longer appear to be an "exhaustible-resource" limit on the supply of raw energy. Unlimited high-cost nuclear energy can be used to produce larger quantities of other forms of high-cost energy such as hydrogen, shale oil, and liquefied coal. The economic problems will be to find the capital for investment in facilities and to protect the environment, which has a limited carrying capacity against the effects of nuclear generation.

In trying to "model" the future economic growth of the United States, which is what economists are occupationally prone to do, we can assume a high-cost backstop for nuclear energy after a certain date, with high investment requirements but a very elastic supply of energy if prices rise to the necessary levels. We can also assume a transitional period, during which prices rise steeply above 1970 levels as conventional petroleum is depleted, switching over at some point to a much less steep rise in real costs as coal comes on as the chief base of the energy system, and eventually switching to a highly elastic, but high-level, cost gradient if nuclear energy takes over. Alternative assumptions about the switchover points, the heights of the thresholds, the elasticities of the supply functions, and the resource endowments of the fossil fuels available to the United States can be plugged into alternate models.

One other supply parameter, somewhat akin to a "backstop" element, has to be included in U.S. energy modeling: the price of foreign oil in the United States. This parameter may be relevant only for the next twenty or twenty-five years, if world supplies are indeed being depleted rapidly. The most plausible assumption is that the price of foreign oil will remain high, that it will move upward from a 1970 base, carrying domestic oil prices with it, until a switchover price zone for a coal-based energy economy is reached. But if foreign oil prices for some reason do not behave that way—if world supply should turn out to be much more abundant than we now expect and if the OPEC monopoly should collapse, leading to much lower world oil prices—then the United States might get more of its energy from that cheaper source, if it can adequately safeguard its security while doing so. The backstop would be pushed back in time, unless, of course, the United States should put an arbitrary floor under domestic energy prices and limit oil imports to forestall those effects. In any event, when modeling U.S. energy and growth, we have to make some assumptions about world oil supply, the prices to be fixed by OPEC, and U.S. policy toward oil imports.

Some Findings

Several models of the energy future have recently been

published. They are based on different sets of expectations
and structural assumptions. We need not dwell on the details.
Each considers the process of growth in relation to energy
supplies, which in turn result from investment in energy production constrained by resource endowments. They incorpo-
rate technological change and growth in the labor supply in
various ways.

1. *The Nordhaus model,* published by the Brookings
Institution, projects energy consumption and production
patterns over the next forty years and more.[11] Ultimately
supplies of energy resources are assumed to be fixed. The
model takes as given the quantities of usable energy needed
and thus leaves some substitution of other inputs for energy
out of the picture. It predicts early exhaustion of proved
petroleum reserves and increasing dependence on imported
petroleum to about the year 2000, with a transition to a
world energy market increasingly dominated by U.S. coal and
shale oil after 2020 or so. Transition to nuclear technology—
the ultimate backstop—occurs through the twenty-first century. Real energy prices (1970 dollars) are expected to rise
over the next forty years, by which time oil will be approach-
ing exhaustion. (No solution is provided for the security
problem during the remaining decades of the twentieth century, but Nordhaus finds that if oil imports were cut off
during that period, overall energy costs to the U.S. economy
would increase by about 50 percent.)

This investigation did not try to measure the effect of
higher energy prices on growth by incorporating them into an
input-output model or a model of growth. But the predicted
changes in energy prices (up to five times 1970 levels by
2010) are evidently not so great as to cause growth to come
to a halt; we are already nearly at three times that level. Nor
is it probable that exhaustion of energy resources will make it
impossible to continue to operate our advanced industrial
economy over the long run. Nordhaus does not, of course,
provide solutions for short-term disturbances during energy

transitions. But the long-run view is optimistic.

2. *The Hudson-Jorgenson model.* Edward A. Hudson and Dale W. Jorgenson have constructed a more elaborate model of energy growth patterns to 2000 (reported in the *Bell Journal* and in the final report of the Ford Foundation Energy Policy Project).[12] It is a model of the entire U.S. economy for about the next fifty years. It gives special attention to the role that energy plays in the economy, both as an input to industrial processes and as a final consumption good.

In the Ford Foundation version, the model is run for several different assumptions about energy availability and supply elasticities. In the "technical fix" scenario, prices of fuel inputs are expected to increase markedly, with electricity prices more than doubling by 2000 as a result. But (given time to adjust) the ultimate impact of the higher energy costs on the economy is relatively small. By comparison with what would happen if historical growth rates in energy availability were projected into the future, this "Technical Fix" scenario would result in a U.S. real GNP lower by less than 4 percent in the year 2000 than what GNP would have been without significant energy constraints. The *rate* of growth over that period would be slightly lower by about 0.2 percent per year. Neither would the overall price level be much affected. What *would* be much affected is the use of energy: total energy input would be 38 percent lower in 2000 than it would be if historical growth rates were continued, though GNP would be less than 4 percent lower.[13] There would be no reduction in employment compared to the base case. The main result, then, is that the economy can absorb a major decline in energy use without major dislocation.[14]

These are not exact forecasts of actual events, of course. What the models show is that our economy can conserve energy to a considerable degree in response to price increases, by eliminating waste, replacing existing capital with more energy-efficient capital, substituting nonenergy inputs for energy, and altering the composition of goods and service output without anything like a corresponding reduction of output or growth.

3. I will briefly mention a third model, developed at the University of Texas by Michael Kennedy and Victor Niemeyer. It analyzes growth over the next fifteen years in terms of the conventional two factors of the steady-growth approach: capital and labor. Production of energy requires labor and capital. The current output of goods and services can be consumed or invested in energy or in nonenergy industries. The model differs from others by including foreign trade, in which energy (oil) is imported into the United States in exchange for exports of other kinds of goods and services.[15]

The investigators used a comparative approach. First, a simulation of the economy was based on historical costs of domestic and imported energy—about $3.50 per barrel of oil equivalent. Under these conditions, the predicted rate of growth of GNP was about 3.5 percent per year, which corresponds to historical experience.

They then assumed other "scenarios." The worst was that the price of imported oil rose to four times its 1970 level and that the capital and labor resources needed to produce domestic oil and natural gas increased to five times their historical levels. Under these conditions, the model indicated that the economy would experience a 3.0 percent growth rate over a ten-year horizon; that is, that there would be only a 0.5 percent reduction in the growth rate as a result of these major changes in energy conditions.

What is the explanation for this rather startling result? It is that even at the current high costs for both domestic and foreign sources of energy, the resources needed to meet those costs are still a small fraction of the entire economy. The current and expected U.S. oil import bill is likewise a small proportion of GNP.

Employment

The immediate impact of an energy "crisis" is disruptive. The layoffs in the automobile industry and other activities that were strongly affected by the oil embargo and the sudden jump in prices of 1973-1974 should not, however, be mistaken for a long-run effect. Employment, as such, does *not* depend on cheap energy if time is allowed for the U.S. economy to make the necessary adjustments to constrained supplies and higher prices. Employment is not linked to energy use by any constant coefficients.

We would expect, in fact, that an economy facing steeply rising real prices for energy might generate an *increase* in employment, or more exactly, in the demand for labor. In the past, the U.S. economy has freely substituted energy for labor while reabsorbing the labor in an expanding total production. In the future, expansion is more likely to be in the service industries, and energy-saving techniques may generate expanded demands for labor even though GNP is growing more slowly.[16]

Econometric models of the United States again lead to predictions that much higher energy prices over the next ten to twenty-five years will have little effect on employment—smaller, at least, than if historically low energy prices continue. As in the case of growth in GNP, any adverse employment effects of high prices would become very small as time goes on. Jorgenson and Hudson, for example, actually predict an *increase* in employment of over 1 percent by 2000 if energy prices remain at high levels.[17] The Federal Energy Administration is not quite so optimistic, but its projections show virtually the same rates of growth in employment to 1985 with high-priced oil as with low-priced oil.[18]

Lack of an adverse effect on employment in the long run does not mean that restricted use of energy will have no effect on labor *productivity* or that real wages would not be adversely affected. Perhaps after the preceding spate of optimism we should now add a few cautionary notes.

Some Cautionary Observations

What our economic analysts have said is that energy scarcities are reflected in energy prices and that high energy prices in advanced industrial economic systems need not have very adverse effects on economic growth during the next fifteen to fifty years. But that is not to say that growing energy scarcities have no adverse implications at all. They do.

One is that *any* relative increase in scarcity of an important resource is bound to have some detrimental impact on human welfare. The U.S. economy compensates for a scarcity of energy in part by substituting other things for it in production and consumption, but consumers still would be better off with cheap energy than with expensive energy. The fact that we have a flexible and versatile economy cushions the blow of higher energy prices, but does not eliminate it.

That observation suggests a second qualifier: some economies in the world are *not* flexible and versatile. Leaving aside the countries that are major producers and exporters of energy resources, what happens now to growth and development in the Third World—and the Fourth?

The long-term effects of higher fossil-fuel prices on the developing countries can be considered primarily in terms of their foreign trade. The capacity of those countries to sustain growth depends on their ability to obtain foreign exchange, which they use to purchase from industrial countries the capital goods and technological services needed for growth. Higher prices for imported oil use up larger amounts of this precious foreign exchange.[19]

Economic specialists have concluded that some of the developing countries—the rapidly growing, export-oriented ones—can absorb the burden of much higher oil import prices without suffering great damage to their rate of development. Many of them hope to take a leaf from OPEC's laurels and raise the prices of what *they* export. But the low-income, slow-growing countries with large, often destitute, populations are in a much poorer situation. For these—the Fourth World, perhaps—"the most likely outcome is a stagnation of per capita incomes for the rest of the decade"[20] and beyond, unless they receive large additional infusions of aid from the developed and newly rich countries.[21]

A third qualifier: economics is not everything. Not much has been said so far about political struggles over oil, or the geopolitical consequences of having it or not having it, or the security problem that the United States and its allies may face during the next decade or so. We address the problems of economic growth while recognizing that political problems may easily overshadow or even nullify them.

With time, security in some degree can be attained at some price. It makes sense to take some risks with imports rather than to have the very high domestic prices that would make the United States totally self-sufficient in energy (which would amount to inflicting a permanent embargo on ourselves). Very high prices would have to work primarily by cutting back *demand.* We can protect ourselves to a considerable extent by (1) guaranteeing minimum prices to domestic energy producers, (2) creating standby capacity, (3) having a storage program, and (4) pushing substitute technology.

One must also remember that frantic development of domestic oil and gas to make us self-sufficient in *petroleum* by 1980 or 1985 shifts the depletion curve forward in time and guarantees that we will be *less* self-sufficient in oil later on. This policy has been called "Drain America First."

Finally, the kind of "long run" we have been talking about is from fifteen to one hundred years, with a primary focus on the rest of the twentieth century. That is not the kind of long run that some of the futurists worry about: their gaze is fixed on a time span of as much as several centuries or even more. They are concerned with the *ultimate* depletion of depletable resources, which is inescapable if one remembers the second law of thermodynamics. Energy cannot be conserved beyond the rate of entropy. The question is, of course, the effect that entropy should have upon conservation of energy now. How should we modify our present activity in view of the fact that resources will eventually be used up?

Before we can answer that, we must ask how far into the future we can see with any confidence. Lacking any strong moral principle for determining the distribution of income between present and future, we look to the calculus of economic values to tell us how economic resources ought to be used over a time when technology is changing rapidly and the future is highly uncertain. We have often been very wrong in making forecasts, but we have to act on the best information we have when decisions are made. Corporations, governments, and the Sierra Club—all have to use the same facts.

It may appear that we, by using up scarce and exhaustible resources, love our children and grandchildren 10 percent per annum less than we love ourselves. But the process does not necessarily work out that way. Our ancestors may have denied themselves things that we now consider necessities in order to invest enough to create an unseemly affluence for us, and we in turn could live very austerely now in order to make possible a fourth vacation trip to Mars for some unseen great-grand-child. We want to avoid pauperizing our remote descendants, who will have no recourse but to dig up our graves and desecrate our tombs. At the same time, we want to avoid the error of a Comanche sage, who while sitting unsuspectingly on the Permian Basin oil province might have counseled his tribe to reduce their consumption of buffalo meat in order to conserve the scarce supplies of arrowhead flint for future generations. And that was only a hundred-odd years ago.

Conclusion

We began with a comparison between the Malthusian outlook on economic growth and the balanced-growth school.

The economists reviewed here are obviously still persuaded that the balanced-growth view of the development process is the correct one. What the energy "crisis" has done is to change some of the parameters. The growing scarcities of energy and other depletable resources in the future are reflected in expected higher real prices—some substantially higher. But, in the Western world at least, that is not likely to bring economic growth to a halt, for as long as we can confidently foresee. In this part of the world, the Malthusians have not been good prophets, and the neo-Malthusians probably are no better.

Notes

1. This chapter is substantially reprinted, with modifications, from the *Proceedings: International Ex-Students' Conference on Energy,* University of Texas at Austin, April 26-30, 1976, pp. 187-195, where it appeared under the title, "Energy and Economic Growth." The Center for Energy Studies has given permission to reprint. I wish to acknowledge the collaboration of Drs. Michael Kennedy and E. Victor Niemeyer of the University of Texas at Austin. Readers wishing to pursue the question further are referred to Michael Kennedy and E. Victor Niemeyer, "A Model of Energy and Economic Growth," *Proceedings,* pp. 196-201. Available from the Center for Energy Studies, the University of Texas at Austin, Austin, Texas 78712.

2. During the fifty-year period 1920-1970, the energy consumption of the U.S. economy per dollar of GNP in constant prices fell at first and then stabilized. We used 141,000 Btu per dollar of GNP in 1920, but only 95,000 Btu in 1970. Meanwhile, U.S. energy use per capita rose from 186 million Btu in 1920 to 335 million Btu in 1970. Joel Darmstadter, "Energy Consumption: Trends and Patterns," in *Energy, Economic Growth, and the Environment* (Baltimore and London: Johns Hopkins University Press for Resources for the Future, 1972), Table 1, p. 158. In 1968 the entire world consumed 55 million Btu per capita—about one-sixth the U.S. rate of use. The figure for South Asia was only 7½ million Btu per capita. Ibid., Table 9, p. 179.

3. See, for example, Edwin Burmeister and A. Rodney Dobell, *Mathematical Theories of Economic Growth* (New York: The Macmillan Co., 1970), Chapter 2.

4. Donella H. Meadows; Dennis L. Meadows; Jørgen Randers; and William W. Behrens III, *The Limits to Growth: A Report for the Club of Rome's Project on the Predicament of Mankind,* (New York: Signet, 1972).

5. See, for example, Herman E. Daly, ed., *Toward a Steady-State Economy* (San Francisco: W. H. Freeman and Co., 1973); Edward F. Renshaw, *The End of Progress* (North Scituate, Mass.: Duxbury Press, 1976).

6. William Nordhaus and James Tobin, "Is Growth Obsolete?" in *Economic Growth,* National Bureau of Economic Research, Fiftieth Anniversary Colloquium V (New York: Columbia University Press, 1972), p. 16.

7. See, for example, M. King Hubbert, *Resources and Man* (Washington: National Academy of Sciences, 1969).

8. John Steinhart of the University of Wisconsin, reported in the *Wall Street Journal,* March 25, 1976.

9. U.S., Congress, Senate, Committee on Interior and Insular Affairs, *Conservation of Energy,* 92d Cong., 2d sess., serial no. 92-18.

10. Cf. William D. Nordhaus, "The Allocation of Energy Resources," *Brookings Papers on Economic Activity,* no. 3 (1973), pp. 532, 547-548.

11. Ibid.

12. E. A. Hudson and D. W. Jorgenson, "U.S. Energy Policy and Economic Growth, 1975-2000," *The Bell Journal of Economics and Management Sciences* Autumn 1974, pp. 461-514; Ford Foundation, *A Time to Choose* (Cambridge, Mass.: Ballinger Publishing Co., 1974), Appendix F, "Economic Analysis of Alternative Energy Growth Patterns, 1975-2000," pp. 493-511.

13. Energy input would increase from 78 quadrillion Btu in 1975 to 115 quadrillion Btu, rather than to 185 quadrillion Btu by 2000, as it would if past conditions continue into the future.

14. Ford Foundation, *A Time to Choose,* p. 501.

15. See note 1 for references to the published source of the full model.

16. Herman A. Daly, "Electric Power, Employment, and Economic Growth," in Daly, *Toward a Steady-State Economy,* especially pp. 260-263.

17. In the "technical fix" scenario. Ford Foundation, *A Time to Choose,* p. 494.

18. In both cases, employment growth 1973-1985 is projected at 1.5 percent per year. U.S., Federal Energy Administration, *Project Independence Report* (Washington, D.C.: Government Printing Office,

1974), Table VI-2, p. 320.

19. Wouter Tims, "The Developing Countries," in *Higher Oil Prices and the World Economy: The Adjustment Problem,* ed. Edward R. Fried and Charles L. Schultze (Washington, D.C.: The Brookings Institution, 1975).

20. Ibid., p. 195.

21. Fried and Schultze, "Overview," in ibid., p. 38.

3
Intercountry Comparisons of Energy Use: Any Lessons for the United States?

Joel Darmstadter

Discussions of energy conservation potentials in the United States have frequently taken note of the lower levels of per capita energy consumption prevailing in other industrialized countries and have given rise to the assertion—or, at least, implication—that these foreign examples validate the case for energy conservation in this country.[1]

A recently completed effort to disentangle some of the factors accounting for intercountry differences in energy use patterns finds that things are more complex than, rhetorically, they are sometimes made out to be.[2] The remarks in this chapter draw largely upon research done at Resources for the Future, though they also reflect the findings of some other research efforts.[3]

For the United States to manifest what appear to be the energy-conserving characteristics of, say, an industrialized West European economy, one or both of two conditions would have to be met. First, the United States would have to have an economic, social, and demographic complexion sufficiently similar to the "model" country to validate the comparison; otherwise, we are comparing apples and oranges. Second, in those cases where similar economic or societal activities—say, driving, home heating, or manufacturing processes—are managed with less energy input than in the United States, then the U.S. public, policymakers, or industrial managers must take a hard look at, and consider adopting, those measures governing that restrained energy use. When this additional, but indispensable, step is taken, Americans do not always seem to like what they find—e.g., the much higher motor fuel taxes prevailing in other countries.

But before proceeding with more specific aspects of inter-country comparisons, let me briefly touch on some basic issues and concepts. Energy use has tended to show a rather strong positive correlation with overall economic activity, judging from the historical experience of different countries as well as from multicountry, cross-sectional circumstances at any given time. But a strong positive correlation between energy consumption and economic activity by no means implies that a given percentage change in national output is associated with an identical percentage change in energy consumption. The United States, for example, saw energy consumption rise more steeply than GNP in the closing decades of the nineteenth century and in the early part of the twentieth. By contrast, for the greater part of the period since the 1920s, U.S. energy consumption, on the average, grew at only two-thirds the annual rate of GNP growth—a phenomenon that, incidentally, accompanied a long-term *decline* in energy prices relative to other prices.

Apart from the fact that a generally high correlation between economic activity and energy consumption fails to define the respective rates of change ("elasticities") of these two forces, a close look at the quantitative record discloses, moreover, numerous specific exceptions to general trend relationships. These exceptions, dramatically revealed when one compares patterns of energy use and economic activity among different countries, do invite serious thinking about whether there may not be considerable flexibility in future U.S. energy consumption levels, whatever level of national output materializes. The lessons drawn from international experience may thus reinforce judgments emerging from other evidence and analysis about the scope for such flexibility.

Simply stated, the U.S. per capita consumption of energy resources is considerably higher than that of several other advanced industrial countries—e.g., France, Germany, Sweden—whose per capita income or output levels cluster within a range not appreciably different from that of the United States. Consequently, the U.S. energy/output ratio exceeds by a considerable margin the ratio in many other countries. (But Canada's ratio is even higher.) Why is this so? The importance of the question, as indicated, is obvious. For if something close to the U.S. standard of living were found to be compatible with a fraction of the prevailing level of energy use, that finding could have an important impact on the direction of U.S. energy conservation and supply development strategies. The data shown in the following multicountry tabulation (Table 3.1) deserve therefore a careful look. In Table 3.1, we use gross domestic product (GDP) as our national output measure: it is virtually identical to gross national product (GNP) for most countries, but it is the preferred indicator for energy consumption comparisons because it excludes that part of a country's income arising from foreign investments.

In interpreting intercountry energy/output variability, and particularly in considering the applicability of the findings to the United States, we need to probe the underlying reasons for such differences. Thus, we want to know whether the variability is primarily the consequence of the energy intensity that characterizes given activities within the respective economies or whether it arises from the fact that there are important "structural" (or "mix") differences among the countries. Aggregated energy/GDP comparisons may obscure structural factors highly relevant to the analysis, because it is possible for one country to have a much higher energy/GDP rate ratio than another solely because of the predominance of inherently energy-intensive activities, e.g., chemicals or metallurgy. Thus, the fact that the ratio for Canada is even higher than that for the United States arises in large part from the

TABLE 3.1

Per Capita Energy Consumption and Per Capita Gross Domestic Product, Nine Developed Countries, 1972

Country	Per capita GDP (dollars)	Per capita Energy (barrels oil equivalent)	Energy/GDP ratio (barrels oil equivalent per $ thousand)	Index numbers (US=100) Per capita GDP	Index numbers (US=100) Per capita Energy	Index numbers (US=100) Energy/GDP ratio
United States	5,643	61.0	10.8	100	100	100
Canada	4,728	61.2	12.9	84	100	120
France	4,168	24.2	5.8	74	40	54
Germany	3,991	30.1	7.5	71	49	70
Italy	2,612	17.4	6.7	46	29	62
Netherlands	3,678	34.2	9.3	65	56	86
United Kingdom	3,401	27.8	8.2	60	46	76
Sweden	5,000	38.8	7.8	89	64	72
Japan	3,423	21.2	6.2	61	35	57

NOTE:

The hydro and nuclear component of primary energy consumption is converted into Btu's on the basis of fuel inputs into fossil-fueled power plants, assuming 35 percent efficiency. Foreign GDPs are expressed in dollars, using a real purchasing-power basis of comparison rather than market exchange rates.

preponderance of such industries. On the other hand, Sweden's ratio is lower in spite of a more energy-intensive manufacturing sector.

Both the structural and the energy-intensity characteristics of an economy may be only the surface manifestations of more deep-seated features—e.g., geography, resource endowment, technology, demographic factors, and economic policies—to which comparative analysis must address itself. For instance, a country may have a comparative advantage in steelmaking, including the ability to export steel to countries lacking that capacity, because it has abundant coal and iron ore deposits—scarcely circumstances betraying energy profligacy. On the other hand, a country may keep its energy consumption below what it would otherwise be because of such policy decisions as mandatory insulation standards, taxation of motor fuels and excessive automotive horsepower, or subsidization of public transport facilities.

The findings summarized in Table 3.1 above reflect a number of these elements, which, furthermore, apply in different degree to the various economic sectors of the nine countries included. A few comments on the comparative factors lying behind these tabulated aggregates may therefore be instructive.

When national economic activity and energy use in each country are broken down into principal consuming sectors— residential/commercial, transport, industry—it turns out that by far the greatest portion of intercountry differences in energy/GDP ratios is due to transportation. Not only are U.S. passenger cars about 50 percent more energy-intensive (in terms of fuel per passenger mile) than European cars, but relative to given income levels, Americans also travel a lot more than Europeans. Indeed, this factor is quantitatively more important than automotive energy intensity in explaining why the United States devotes far more energy to transportation than Western Europe does. Since Americans generate a greater proportion of their passenger miles in urban rather than in intercity highway traffic—compared with, say, Sweden—the tendency for lower U.S. fuel economy is reinforced. A third factor is the proportionately greater share of less energy-intensive public transport modes in the foreign energy mix. These differences are the result not only of the much higher cost (because of taxes) of acquiring and operating cars abroad. They are also associated with urban density differentials between the United States and other countries and with public policy measures resulting, overseas, in highly subsidized public transport. From a policy standpoint, and especially in a ten-year or twenty-year time span, it may be far more promising to work toward greatly enhanced efficiency of automobiles than to strive, in a major way, for the kinds of travel characteristics and mass transit reliance that still prevail abroad. It is worth noting, however, that in almost all advanced countries except Japan, cars are overwhelmingly the dominant passenger transport mode.

Freight transport also contributes to the higher U.S. energy/GDP ratio. Interestingly, this comes about exclusively by virtue of the high volume of traffic, relative to GDP, that is generated in the United States compared to traffic in the grouping of European countries that were analyzed. Indeed, the United States freight modal mix is, more than Western Europe's, oriented to such energy-saving forms as rail, pipelines, and waterborne traffic. If one argues that size of country and long-distance haulage of bulk commodities, such as ores, grains, and coal, are inherent characteristics of the U.S. economic structure and geography, then a relatively high U.S. energy/GDP ratio for freight is in no obvious way reflective of comparative energy "inefficiency." In a comparison of freight movement within urban areas only, Sweden recorded less energy-intensive characteristics.

Intercountry differences in industrial energy use also contribute to the higher overall energy/GDP ratio for the United States. The industrial contribution to higher U.S. energy use occurs notwithstanding the fact that our industrial sector is proportionately smaller than elsewhere. But the United States exhibits more energy-intensive production processes.

Indeed, if industrial value added were as high a proportion of U.S. national output as it is in most foreign countries, U.S. energy consumption would be still higher. What is true for the industrial sector as a whole appears to be the case also in a diverse number of specific manufacturing segments. For example, Swedish manufacturing industries actually turn out *more* energy-intensive industrial materials, as a percentage of total dollar output and energy use, than is the case in the United States. But product for product, output is generally less energy-intensive in Sweden than in the United States. This appears to be because Swedish technology is newer and optimized by virtue of considerably higher fuel prices.

One should perhaps add that differences between the United States and other countries in industrial energy intensity need not inevitably reflect differences in the *overall efficiency* of carrying on a given industrial operation. To articulate the relationship between energy intensity and economic efficiency, one would need to explore, in addition to the cost of energy resources, such "inputs" as labor, capital, and nonenergy materials. But the findings, as far as they go, constitute at least a strong presumption that U.S. industrial managers concerned with energy utilization might profitably look at foreign practices and results.

U.S. households are, relative to income, bigger energy consumers than their foreign counterparts, even *after* adjustment for climate. In part, this arises from the need to provide space heating and cooling for larger, single-family homes. But it is also due to such practices—historically facilitated by relatively cheap fuel prices—as the heating of unoccupied rooms and the maintenance of higher temperatures. Compared to Canada and Sweden, U.S. insulation practices are inferior. For example, at given "degree days," and relative to areas of living space, Sweden appears to consume half as much energy as the United States in space heating.

I have mentioned the impact of differential prices and
taxes on comparative energy use. But nonprice policy and
technological factors should also be noted. For example,
Swedish weatherization standards for buildings, when combined with generous mortgage allowances for energy conservation investments, have allowed for economy in the use of heat.
In several foreign countries, thermal generation of electric
power combines heat and electricity production in industries
or in communities where the "reject" heat is used as industrial
process steam or "district heat" for multifamily residences.
Although U.S. locational patterns in both homes and factories
may not be suitable for extensive district heating—because of
heat losses in trying to serve dispersed consumption centers—
the energy savings from this practice are so impressive that
its possible use in this country deserves a close look.

In the years ahead, new conditions of energy supply and
costs, new policies, and new attitudes on conservation and
the environment may significantly alter some of the historic
U.S. energy use patterns; indeed, some of the characteristics
of energy use overseas may begin to appear here. More economic automotive practices and space conditioning improvements seem clear-cut candidates for enhanced energy utilization. Some notable gains in reducing unit energy requirements in a number of U.S. industrial activities appear to have
taken place since 1973-1974. But more appropriate economic
signals to energy users are probably a key ingredient in fash-
ioning a U.S. energy picture more nearly like that elsewhere. Certainly, other countries have made much more
resourceful use—both before and after the 1973 Arab-Israeli
war—of the price and tax instruments that influence energy-
associated consumption practices.

No tidy final reckoning is possible on these questions.
The research I have summarized here points to complex and
diverse reasons for intercountry differences in energy consumption. Variations in energy/output ratios should not in

themselves be viewed as indicators either of economic efficiency or even of energy efficiency. Economic efficiency depends on how energy is used in combination with other resources, particularly capital and labor, and the relative costs of all of these. National energy/output ratios also depend critically on the composition of a country's output, not merely on the energy intensities associated with these component products and activities.

Some of these compositional differences—for example, automotive patterns—appear to be decisively influenced by relative user costs. Changes in these costs might significantly alter energy consumption practices. Other notable differences, such as suburbanization, housing, and mobility characteristics, each with marked influence on energy use, might arguably owe some of their historic momentum to cheap energy in the United States and costly levels elsewhere, but they are clearly related to many other impelling forces as well. Whatever their origins, some of these features have become such firmly established elements in U.S. society that it would be unrealistic to expect dramatic change or reversal, even in an era of new energy prices. Viewed in this way, energy consumption is, in many of its aspects, essentially a by-product or, at best, only one element within the wider framework of societal arrangements and choices.

In sum, international experience and our own economic history suggest that the energy consumption required to provide society with a given set of amenities may display considerable flexibility. But thinking that assumes that an energy-conservation ethic and abhorrence of waste are present "over there" and lacking in the United States is at odds with the facts and is simplistic in its view of the world. The need to proceed with energy conservation strategies appropriate to the United States is too urgent a task to allow ourselves to be too much transfixed by a foreign yardstick that, though intermittently revealing, can also be illusory.

Notes

1. This text is a slightly altered version of the author's testimony on April 4, 1977, before the Subcommittee on Advanced Energy Technologies and Energy Conservation Research, Development and Demonstration, Committee on Science and Technology, U.S. House of Representatives.

2. J. Darmstadter, J. Dunkerley, and J. Alterman, *How Industrial Societies Use Energy: A Comparative Analysis.* A preliminary report covering major findings is available from Resources for the Future, 1755 Massachusetts Ave. N.W., Washington, D.C. 20036.

3. For example, Lee Schipper and Allen Lichtenberg, "Efficient Energy Use and Well Being: The Swedish Example," *Science,* December 3, 1976.

4
U.S. Energy Conservation

L. G. Rawl

I appreciate the invitation from Bob Burch to discuss the potential for energy conservation in the United States with such a distinguished group.

Within Exxon, we have for several years been making assessments of the total U.S. energy environment ten to fifteen years in the future; these are essential for our long-term business plans and investment decisions. The general conclusion from these "outlooks" is that the solution to the U.S. energy problem will require both the accelerated development of *all* domestic energy resources *and* increased energy conservation.

I will use our latest *Energy Outlook,* which was developed in February 1977, as a framework for discussing the potential for energy conservation and the continuing urgent need for rapid development of the U.S. energy supply potential.

U.S. Energy Demand by Consuming Sector

As background to the discussion, Figure 4.1 summarizes the projection of total energy demand by consuming sectors through 1990. It will be used to make some general points about energy demand and conservation before getting into more detail on the potential for conservation within the vari-

Figure 4.1

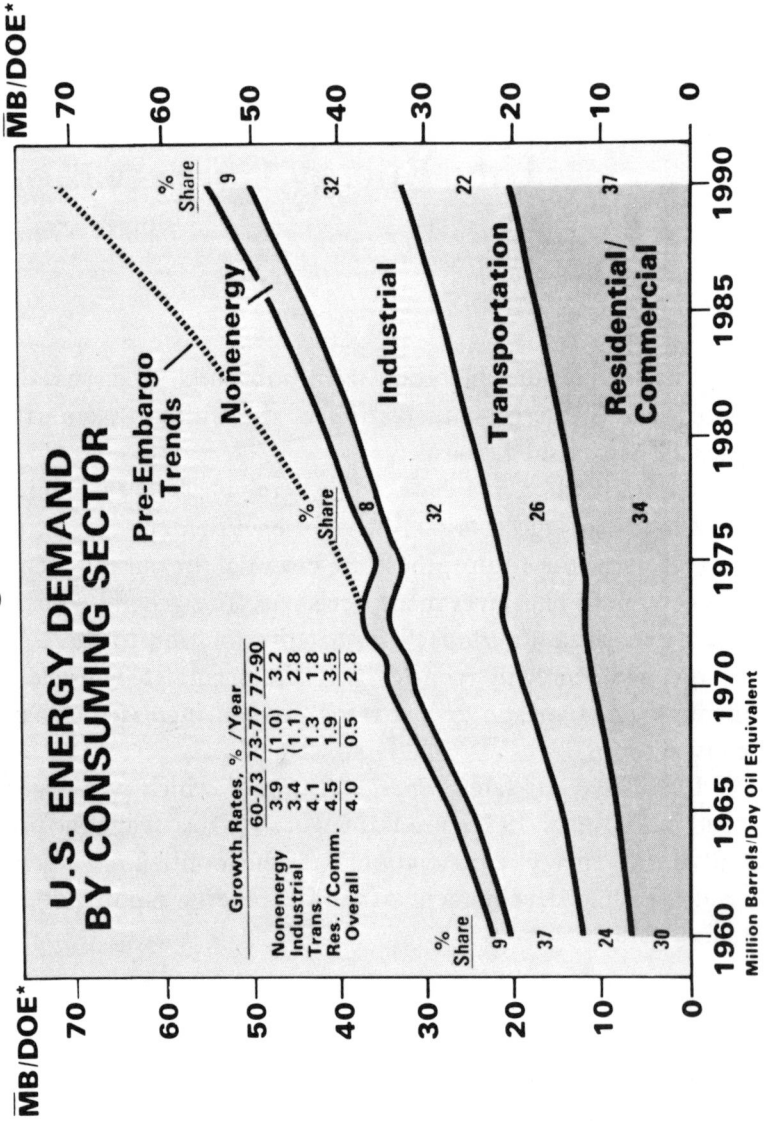

U.S. ENERGY DEMAND BY CONSUMING SECTOR

ous use categories. The vertical scale is in millions of barrels per day of oil equivalent (mmb/doe). A barrel of oil *equivalent* is merely a convenient measure of all forms of energy in terms of their heat content relative to that of oil.

As illustrated by the small table in the upper left of Figure 4.1, we projected in February 1977 an energy demand growth of less than 3 percent per year between now and 1990 as compared with the 4 percent annual growth rate of the 1960-1973 period.

The lower-than-historic energy growth rate in the *Outlook* is due partly to lower-than-historic economic growth and partly to a substantial amount of energy conservation. The rate of economic growth, of course, is a key factor in projecting energy demand. We estimate the long-term growth trend in gross national product (GNP) will be about 3.5 percent per year, as contrasted to an average annual growth rate of more than 4 percent in the 1960-1973 period. This lower growth rate is due to a slowing of growth in the labor force, a slightly lower rate in productivity growth, and a slightly higher base unemployment level.

The second reason for the lower-than-historic energy growth rate is that the *Outlook* projects a substantial amount of conservation to occur between now and 1990. In order to evaluate and measure the level of conservation in the *Outlook,* it was first necessary to develop a reference case, which we call the "pre-embargo trends continue" projection. This reference case projects what total energy demand would have been if we had used today's outlook for future economic growth but assumed that energy use patterns and energy prices—in real dollar terms—remained at their 1972 levels.

This "trends continue" projection is the dashed upper line on Figure 4.1. The actual demand level in our February *Outlook* is represented by the top solid line. The interval between these two lines implies a conservation savings equivalent to about 18 mmb/d of oil by 1990, which is about 25 percent less than the "pre-embargo trends continue" projection.

Moreover, the *Outlook* projects that this conservation will occur in all consuming sectors. Looking at each sector, as given by the growth rate table on Figure 4.1, we see that residential/commercial growth slows to 3.5 percent per year from the previous 4.5 percent per year. Conservation resulting from a vast aggregation of individual consumer actions, including less use of energy-consuming devices as well as expenditures for more efficient facilities, is expected to reduce demand in 1990 by 25 percent, almost 7 million barrels a day oil equivalent (mmb/doe), below previous trends.

Transportation energy growth is projected at less than half the historic rate. The growth rate trend in this sector is heavily dominated by the automobile, where mandated fuel efficiency standards are projected to depress the gasoline demand growth rate. The transportation sector will still be using about 12 mmb/d of oil in 1990, but this is almost 4 mmb/d, or 23 percent, below the "trends continue" projection.

The industrial sector growth rate is also down, with conservation expected to reduce 1990 demand by over 7 mmb/doe, or 30 percent below the previous trend. This will come about through better management to reduce operating costs by the elimination of waste in existing facilities, by retrofitting facilities and replacing worn-out units with more efficient equipment, and by the development and use of new industrial processes that are more energy-efficient.

Finally, in what we have labeled the nonenergy sector, demand is expected to grow at about 3.2 percent per year in the future versus almost a 4 percent annual rate in the past. Consumers in this sector use oil, gas, and metallurgical coal as feedstock or raw material rather than as fuel to manufacture such items as petrochemicals, lubricants, and asphalts. Reduction in the growth rate stems from indirect conservation—slower growth in product demand because of the higher energy cost component in the product price—as well as from more saturated market conditions for some chemical products.

As mentioned earlier, the conservation effects by 1990 in the four consuming sectors total nearly 18 mmb/doe, which is more than the total oil consumed in the United States in 1976.

But the easy part of energy conservation is talking about it. Accomplishing the levels in the *Outlook* will be difficult and will come about slowly. We must recognize that this conservation has to result from many millions of individual decisions, most of which will be contrary to habits of long standing. There is a huge capital stock of energy-using devices, which represent a very sizable fraction of the private wealth of this country. These assets will be used more efficiently and ultimately replaced with more efficient assets under normal market mechanisms. Actions to accelerate this process must recognize that considerable potential exists for distortions and dislocations in the overall economy.

Conservation occurs by two general types of actions. The first is simply reduced use of energy, such as not driving as much as you used to, or turning off unnecessary lights. The second type of action is more efficient use of energy, which simply means the obtaining of more useful work from a given amount of energy. An example of this is the improved miles per gallon the average 1977 model car gets versus the average 1973 model car.

Although it is very difficult to measure precisely how much conservation results from each of these two types, the next three figures do give a feel for what is involved in changing a nation's energy use patterns. These figures deal with the *technical potential* for conservation—that is, how much more efficient can we make the things that use energy with readily available technology, and how fast can these more efficient units find their way into our homes, offices, and factories? I will also indicate some of the problems of achieving the potential and then tie this potential back to the amount of conservation included in our February *Outlook*.

Potential Conservation in the
Residential/Commercial Sector in 1990

The residential/commercial sector represents the extreme example of the complexity involved in estimating and accomplishing energy conservation. The total bar in Figure 4.2 represents the 1990 "trends continue" projection of 26.7 mmb/doe. Considering only the technical potential, this level could be reduced by more than 6 mmb/doe by three major activities.

Starting at the top, a complete change out of old major and small appliances and lighting could save about 700 mb/doe by 1990. For example, there are about *270 million* major appliances today—stoves, freezers, clothes dryers, and water heaters. By 1990, this number will grow to an estimated *370 million* individual appliances, all of which could be about 20 percent more efficient on the average than today. These units have a useful life of fifteen to twenty years, and although the efficiency improvement is attractive, the amount of energy saved per unit is quite small. Thus, the replacement rates for these appliances will be highly sensitive to how much the individual unit costs relative to the cost of the energy saved by the more efficient unit. Small appliances could be improved about 10 percent, largely as a result of more efficient electric motors. With a useful life of eight to ten years, improved efficiency today will yield gradual, phased-in energy savings. Using fluorescent lighting would produce about four times as much light per watt as do incandescent lamps. However, builders and homeowners have been slow to switch because the initial cost of fluorescent lights is twice as high.

As a second item, Figure 4.2 shows the general area of weatherization of homes. It is estimated that of the nearly *73 million* existing homes in this country, about *58 million* could be improved by some combination of insulation, weather stripping, and utilization of storm doors and win-

85

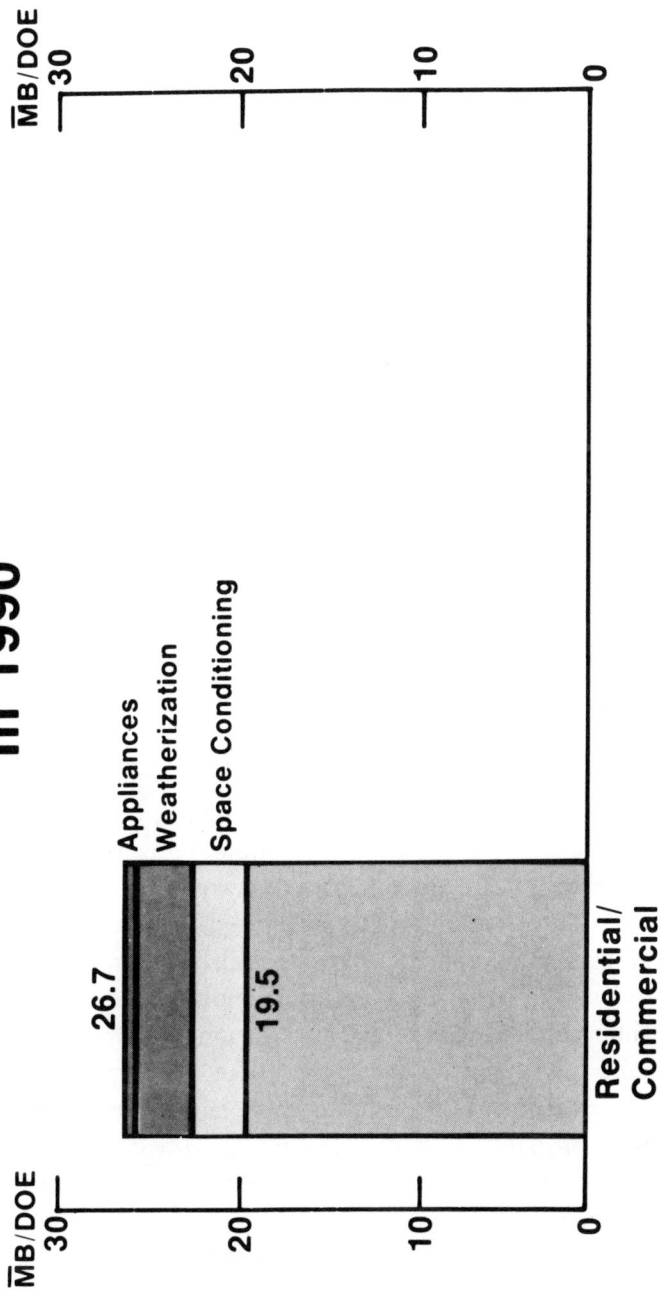

Figure 4.2

Technical Potential Conservation In 1990

dows. If the owners of these 58 million homes make these improvements by 1990, energy demand will be reduced by a substantial amount—2.4 mmb/doe. However, it is obvious that the magnitude of this effort is simply enormous. To give some "gee whizzy" numbers, this effort averages out to over 4,000 insulation jobs per day through 1990, and 11,000 weather stripping jobs per day. I know of no accurate statistics on the existing capacity to accomplish this weatherization work, but there is an obvious potential for cost escalation to offset some of the economic incentives to make these improvements and, thus, prevent or slow achievement of the full potential. In addition, savings of about 950 mb/doe could be achieved by designing and constructing more energy-efficient new homes and buildings.

The third major area is that of space conditioning. Here again, the numbers involved and the magnitude of the task are enormous. About *72 million* central heating units and *23 million* central air units are projected to be in use in the United States by 1990. The use of heat pumps instead of electric resistance heating, electronic ignition instead of pilot lights, and more efficient air conditioning are among a number of design improvements that, if incorporated in probable retrofit applications and in new homes, could save approximately 2 mmb/doe by 1990. These items are generally cost-effective, although heat pumps have the drawbacks of high initial costs and somewhat limited geographic application. Annual maintenance of residential/commercial central heating and cooling units—that is, annual tune-ups and regular filter changes—could save an additional 1.2 mmb/doe. At current costs and energy prices, the economic incentive for annual maintenance is quite small, and getting everyone to do so is probably to expect too much. However, a considerable portion could be realized with better public understanding of the benefit.

Overall, the technical potential for conservation in the residential/commercial sector is estimated to be the equivalent of about 7.2 mmb/d in 1990. Virtually all of it is dependent upon individual actions, which will be highly sensitive to cost and inflation. It would seem probable that a good portion of the retrofit work might price itself out of the market, but be partially offset by reduced use. In 1976, energy use in the residential/commercial sector was already 1.7 mmb/doe below "trends continue." The *Outlook* includes a conservation effect equal to about 92 percent of the technical potential, although a substantial portion of this estimated 6.7 mmb/doe reduction by 1990 is expected to come from reduced use.

Potential Conservation in the
Transportation Sector in 1990

Turning to Figure 4.3, the "trends continue" projection in the transportation sector of nearly 16 mmb/doe can be reduced to about 11 mmb/doe. At the top of the second bar in Figure 4.3, the automobile offers the greatest efficiency potential—3.4 mmb/doe—primarily because it is the sector's largest single consumer of energy. This technical potential results from assuming replacement of essentially all the 100 million cars on the road today by 1990 with the more efficient autos mandated by law. Given an average car life of about ten years, this is not unreasonable. Average new auto mileage was 17.6 miles per gallon (mpg) in 1976 and is required to improve to 20 mpg by 1980 and to 27.5 mpg by 1985.

Improved efficiency of other modes of transportation could save an additional 1.2 mmb/doe. Included in this amount are such items as truck and bus energy use per carrying mile, which could be improved 25 percent through technological and scheduling improvements to save 750 mb/doe in 1990. And if a sustained 65 percent load factor could be attained, 1990 airline energy use could be reduced 150 mb/d from pre-embargo trends.

Figure 4.3

Technical Potential Conservation In 1990

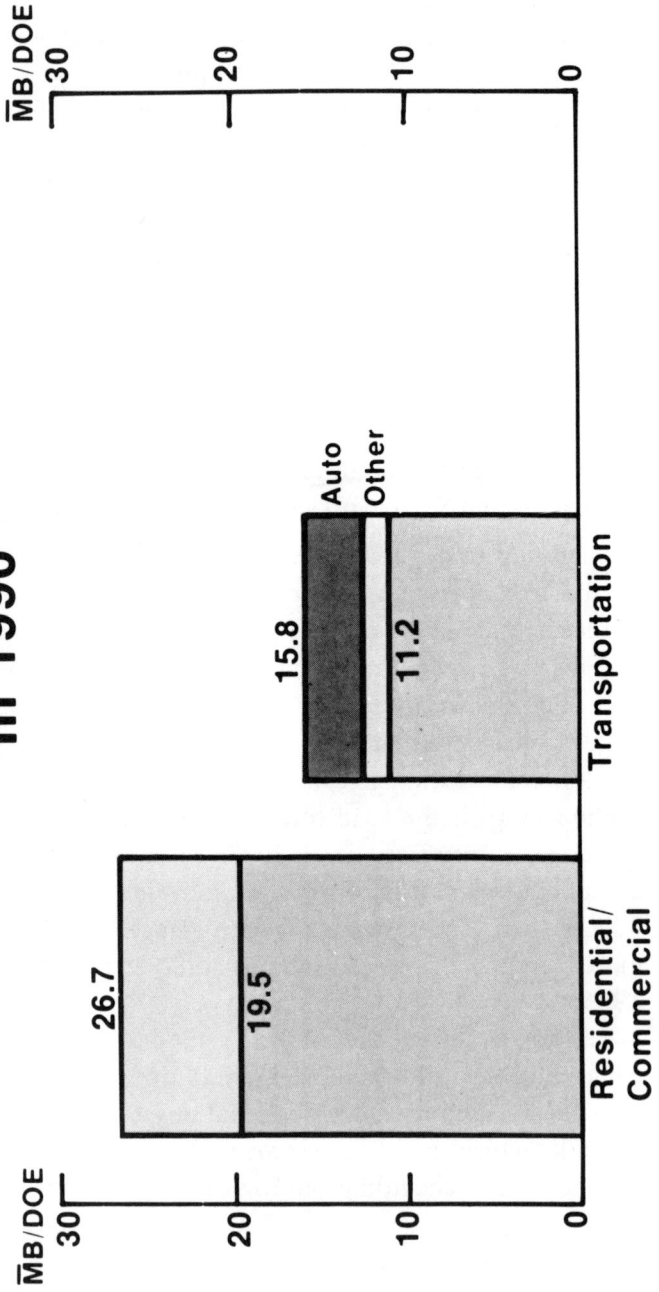

Residential/ Commercial

26.7

19.5

Transportation

Auto

Other

15.8

11.2

$\overline{M}B/DOE$

30

20

10

0

Overall, the technical potential for conservation in the transportation sector is projected to be about 4.6 mmb/doe by 1990. Achieving this potential could require a reversal of the trend toward buying heavier cars. For example, the average weight of today's new car is about 3,500 pounds (the weight of the Ford Granada), and this must be reduced by about 1,000 pounds (to about the weight of a Pinto) to meet the 1985 efficiency target of 27.5 mpg.

There is a very real concern whether the public will adapt quickly to this requirement. This particular *Outlook* assumed that the technical goals required by current law will be somewhat relaxed as time goes by, but that the effects of this relaxation will be offset to some degree by reduced usage influenced by increased gasoline prices. However, should the legislated miles per gallon requirements be reached, then gasoline demand in this *Outlook* would be reduced by an additional 400 mb/d in 1985 and 600 mb/d in 1990.

The *Outlook* projects conservation of 3.7 mmb/doe by 1990, or a little over 80 percent of the potential number. As I indicated, this level of conservation would be increased if the automobile efficiency standards are achieved. Very little of this has taken place to date—about 300 mb/d in 1976. People may be driving a little less and a little slower, but the more efficient cars have not made much of a dent in the total automobile population.

Potential Conservation in the Industrial Sector in 1990

Filling out the picture with a third bar in Figure 4.4, the industrial sector "trends continue" demand of about 25 mmb/doe could be reduced to less than 19 mmb/doe by actions in three general areas. Starting with the top slice of the industrial sector bar, about 1.4 mmb/doe can be saved through better management to reduce energy consumption by eliminating such things as steam leaks and by adjusting lighting

Figure 4.4

Technical Potential Conservation In 1990

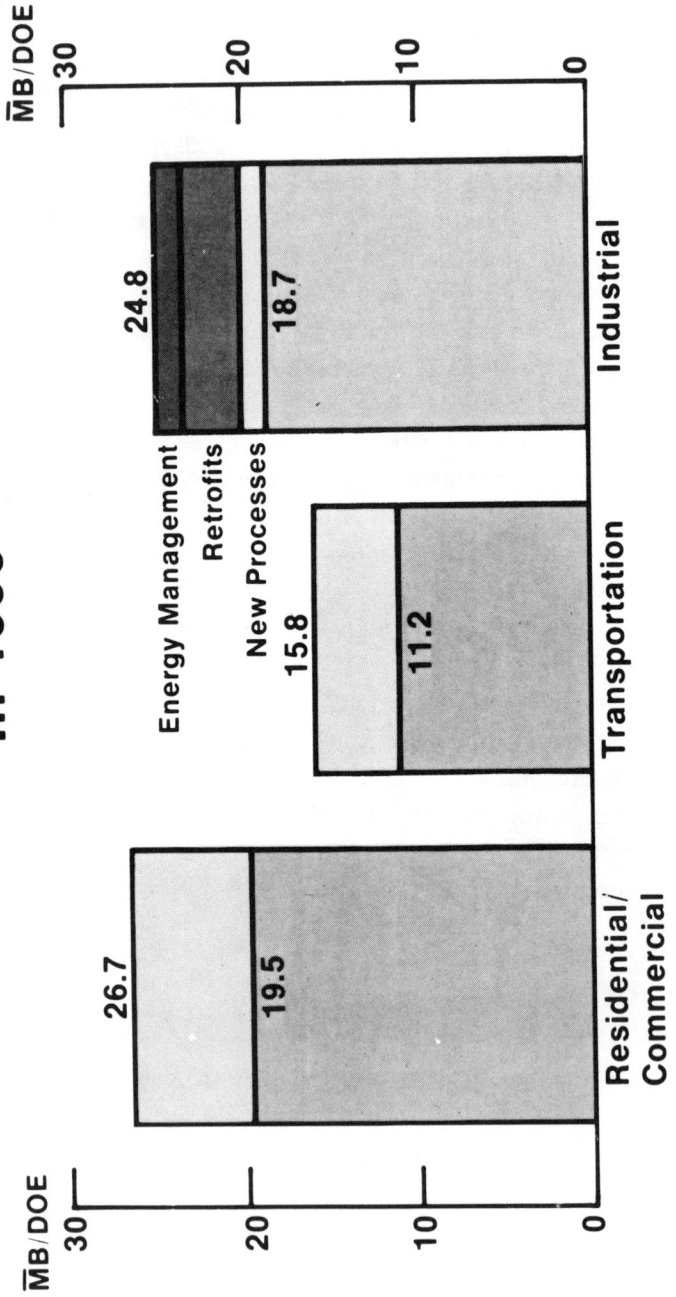

M̄B/DOE

30
20
10
0

Energy Management
Retrofits
New Processes

Industrial
24.8
18.7

Transportation
15.8
11.2

Residential/
Commercial
26.7
19.5

M̄B/DOE

30
20
10
0

and space conditioning to optimum levels. The equivalent of about 3.4 mmb/d could be saved by investment to retrofit existing facilities and replace worn-out facilities with more energy-efficient equipment. For example, current boiler designs are 35-40 percent more efficient than pre-embargo designs (65 percent vs. 90 percent). Retrofitting, normal replacement, and new installations could save 1.8 mmb/doe by 1990. In addition, more efficient new and replacement combustors other than boilers, such as process furnaces, could save another 1.2 mmb/doe by 1990. Another projected saving of 1.4 mmb/doe could come about by using more efficient processes in grass-roots facilities such as continuous casting of steel, which is 5 percent more efficient than the process currently in use in the United States, and dry mixing of cement, which is 14 percent more efficient than wet mixing.

The overall technical potential in the industrial sector is about 6 mmb/doe by 1990. Since conservation in this sector is largely straightforward economics, we expect that all of this 6 mmb/doe will be achieved. In addition, industrial energy production will be further reduced because of reduced product demand related to the higher energy costs. By 1990, an overall 30 percent reduction from pre-embargo trends is projected for the industrial sector. It is estimated that in 1976 industry saved energy equivalent to about 1.8 mmb/d. Much of this probably resulted simply from economically motivated management of how energy is used, but it also probably reflects the results of some of the shorter lead-time efficiency investments.

To summarize this discussion on energy conservation, we see reductions in total energy demand versus a "trends continue" projection of about 18 mmb/doe by 1990. This projection represents rapid and substantial changes in the nation's energy use levels and patterns. Achievement of this reduced demand will involve literally hundreds of millions of individual decisions, many of which are contrary to the consumer's past habits and preferences.

The National Energy Plan, submitted to Congress in April, was positive recognition by the Carter administration that a serious national energy problem exists. It was a clear signal to the public that some hard realities have to be faced in the near future. Combined with realistic energy pricing, this should have the effect of increasing public awareness to the point where meaningful individual actions begin. The National Energy Plan, as you know, is undergoing careful analysis by the various congressional committees in Washington. The latter are making certain changes in it—it is not yet clear exactly what changes—but whatever the final outcome, it should not significantly change the outlook for conservation and energy demand reviewed in this chapter. Energy demand in the National Energy Plan is about 1 percent less in 1985 than in this *Outlook*, which was prepared before April 20, 1977.

However, conservation is only one side of the energy equation. No matter how effective this nation's conservation efforts are, we will be consuming much more energy in 1990 than we do today. Even though conservation is expected to reduce demand by nearly 18 mmb/doe from what it would have been, demand is still projected to increase by 16 mmb/doe over the 1976 level, reaching the range of 54 mmb/doe in 1990. To meet this growing demand, additional energy supplies will be needed.

U.S. Energy Supply

Figure 4.5 looks at energy supplies. This projection assumes an aggressive national policy in energy development and some relaxation of environmental constraints. Hydroelectric and economic geothermal energy are site-limited. Solar energy, though potentially important beyond the *Outlook* period, is currently limited by economic practicality and potential deployment rates. Nuclear energy is projected to develop rapidly. Achieving such development will not be

Figure 4.5

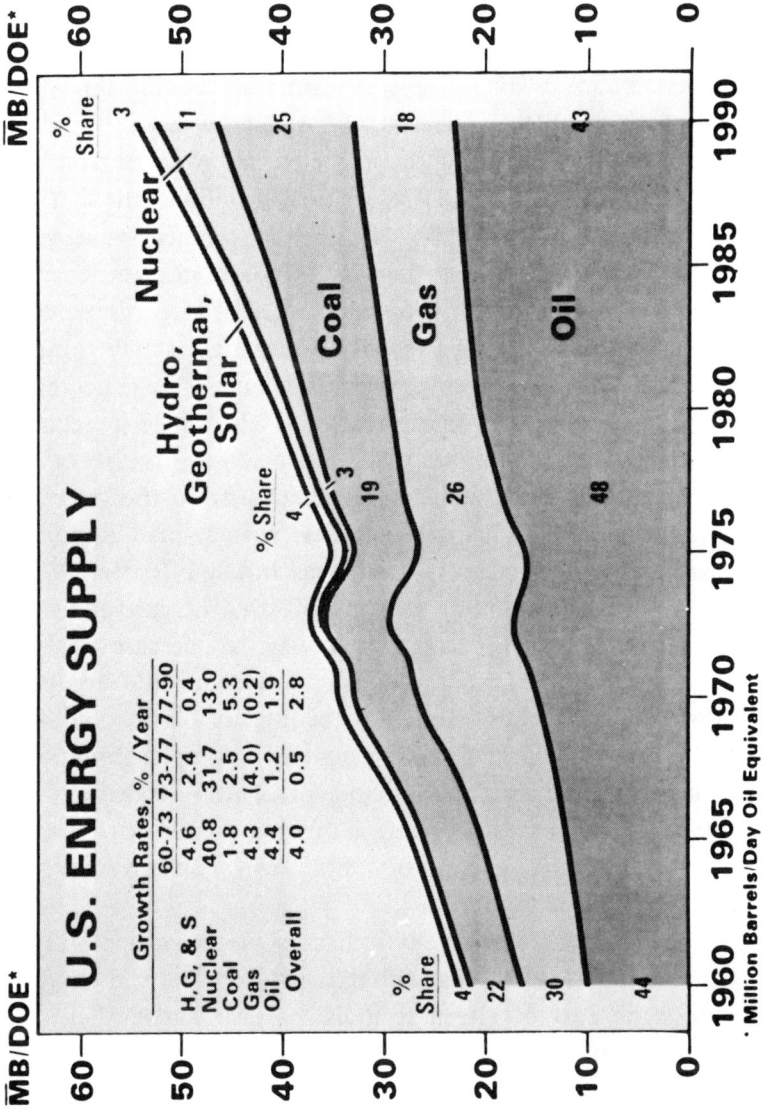

U.S. ENERGY SUPPLY

Growth Rates, %/Year			
	60-73	73-77	77-90
H,G, & S	4.6	2.4	0.4
Nuclear	40.8	31.7	13.0
Coal	1.8	2.5	5.3
Gas	4.3	(4.0)	(0.2)
Oil	4.4	1.2	1.9
Overall	4.0	0.5	2.8

* Million Barrels/Day Oil Equivalent

easy. The nation now has 65 nuclear plants and by 1990 will need 165 more plants, averaging 1000 megawatts in size, to achieve the growth indicated.

Through 1990, coal use is projected to grow at about twice the rate of overall energy demand, reaching almost 1.5 billion tons in 1990. The bulk of this growth will be in the electric utility sector, with projected use growing from 442 million tons (mmt) in 1976 to over a billion tons in 1990, accounting for about half of all electric power generation. After declining for years because of economic and environmental pressures, coal use in the industrial sector is expected to pick up in the 1980s as coal becomes increasingly competitive with alternate fuels. Industrial coal use is expected to amount to over 150 mmt/year in 1990, or 15 percent of industrial fuel requirements. The projected increase in coal use in the *Outlook* will come primarily from the growth in new utility and industrial facilities, with a small amount of coal being converted to synthetic gas and liquids after 1985.

Although converting existing oil-fired or gas-fired facilities to coal appears to offer a way to increase coal use beyond what we have projected, to do so would be uneconomic and, in many cases, not technically feasible. Oil-fired and gas-fired boilers require essentially complete rebuilding to use coal, and the economic penalties increase as the size of the boiler decreases. In many industrial combustors, such as process furnaces, technology does not currently exist to allow coal to be used.

Overall, our assessment indicates that coal use will not expand much faster than what is projected in the *Outlook*, unless the cost of alternate fuels increases substantially. On the other hand, coal use could grow more slowly than projected if environmental restraints are tightened and alternate fuels are available. On the demand side, for example, proposed tighter air quality requirements may preclude using coal in many regions. On the supply side, most of the increased coal production will have to come from large surface mines in the western United States. If new federal strip-mining legislation and procedures frustrate or substantially delay development of these low-sulfur coal reserves, our projection of coal production will not be possible.

In total, coal and nuclear energy sources are expected to supply an increasing fraction of total demand and 70 percent of growth; however, oil and gas must continue to supply the bulk of our energy requirements over this period—61 percent in 1990 versus 75 percent in 1976. To better illustrate a few points in the oil and gas area, the two bottom components of Figure 4.5 are shown on an enlarged scale in Figure 4.6.

U.S. Oil and Gas Supply

As shown in Figure 4.6, total use of oil and gas—expected to be about 33 mmb/doe in 1990—is projected to grow at an average rate of 1.2 percent/year through 1990, only 27 percent of the historic 4.4 percent rate. Imports provide essentially all of the growth in supplies during the *Outlook* period.

There are four sources of future oil and gas supply: imports, synthetics, new domestic discoveries, and production from existing reserves. Two of these, synthetics and production from existing reserves, are probably well fixed in magnitude in this time frame. Synthetics from oil shale and coal, both gas and liquids, are projected at less than 1 mmb/doe in 1990. A maximum case might amount to about 3 million barrels, but even this would be less than 10 percent of demand. Oil and gas production from existing reserves, including extensions and revisions, is expected to continue to decline to about 10 mmb/doe in 1990. Although there may be technology breakthroughs in the area of enhanced recovery, it is not realistic to expect much change in trend in this time frame.

New discoveries are projected to supply 10 mmb/doe through an aggressive exploration and development program. A large fraction of these projected discoveries will be in the

United States Oil And Gas Supply

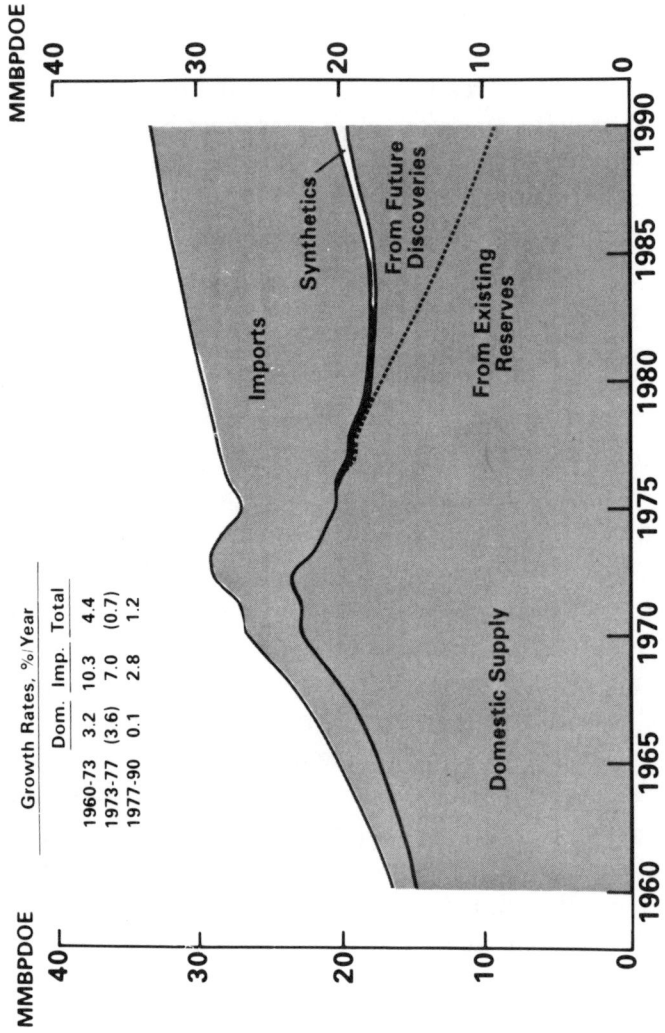

Growth Rates, %/Year

	Dom.	Imp.	Total
1960-73	3.2	10.3	4.4
1973-77	(3.6)	7.0	(0.7)
1977-90	0.1	2.8	1.2

Imports

Synthetics

From Future
Discoveries

From Existing
Reserves

Domestic Supply

MMBPDOE

frontier areas of Alaska and the Outer Continental Shelf (OCS). Any delays in leasing and development activities will make this forecast impossible to achieve.

Today, there appears to be a clear effort not only to slow down leasing activity, but also to redistribute it geographically to reduce its scope. Since no one can know with certainty the amount of oil and gas, if any, that is present in any area until drilling occurs, it would seem to be unwise to preclude at the outset any opportunity to search for potential new discoveries. Moreover, proposed amendments to the OCS Lands Act will delay the development of these areas and substantially reduce the projected domestic production included in the *Outlook.*

The shortfall resulting from these delays would have to be met with increased levels of imports. On the other hand, import levels could be reduced by a more positive and aggressive approach to domestic energy resource development. Looking specifically at the level of imports included in the *Outlook,* it can be seen that despite the projected lower energy demand growth and increases in the supply of other fuels, imports of oil and gas are expected to rise from less than 8 mmb/d last year to almost 13 mmb/d in 1990. Clearly, a concerted effort to develop all energy options aggressively is necessary.

We believe that current and proposed incentives are not adequate to utilize the domestic oil and gas resource base efficiently. The indefinite continuation and expansion of price controls simply do not provide the business climate necessary for conducting the level of energy resource exploration and development needed to achieve optimum utilization of domestic energy resources. Of additional concern is the fact that little or no progress is being made toward removing the barriers that limit access to resources; thus, energy supply development in the United States is held back. These issues must be resolved in order to allow the development of needed domestic energy supplies.

   As the nation's energy policy is debated in the coming months, the importance of developing the supply side of the energy balance equation should not be forgotten. A sound national energy policy should not only encourage conservation, but must also provide a better environment for increased domestic energy production.

5

Coal Schizophrenia, or Be Sure Who Makes the Magic Potion

Richard L. Gordon

Back in 1969, the complaint was that the United States lacked energy policies well designed to attain specific, reasonable goals. Subsequently, both energy market conditions and prevailing public policy have changed greatly. Unfortunately, the alterations have aggravated rather than alleviated the prevailing incoherence.

The president's energy message largely was a failure in properly reorienting public policy. Since Congress has even worse instincts, it can be expected that the actual program enacted will be inferior to the president's. Thus, improvement seems unlikely.

With these considerations in mind, the present paper will appraise a specific defect in energy policy and how the events of 1977 have aggravated the difficulties. In particular, I propose to diagnose a disease that I have named "coal schizophrenia." The essence of this disease is a proclivity to make resounding pronouncements about the need to increase U.S. coal production significantly and then impose regulations severely limiting coal production and use. The practitioners of such policies remind me of Koko's "apologetic statesmen of a compromising kind," whom he put upon his list in *The Mikado*. I similarly follow his advice: "the task of filling up the list, I'd rather leave up to you." I will add, however, that much of the fault of the president's energy message seems due to a clearly conscious restraint from proposing *objectives* unpopular in Congress.[1]

To this theme may be added the second proposition epitomized by suggesting that you be careful about whom you select to provide magic potions. This imagery was inspired by a desire to employ an operatic allusion in honor of our presence at this celebrated music center.[2] In particular, let me call to your attention Dr. Dulcamara, who twice sells a particularly gullible tenor (in Donizetti's *Elixir of Love*) cheap wine as a love potion. Energy discussions have lately been filled with the works of numerous Dulcamaras offering *the answer* to our energy problems. The second basic point, of course, translates into rejection of such views. We simply do not know enough about the determinants of future energy patterns for anyone to forecast with great confidence. Nevertheless, we have good reason to suspect that no single action can, by itself, solve all problems.

For reasons discussed below, all this leads to several conclusions on coal: it *should* play a significant role in U.S. energy; public policy restraints have been overdone; but predictions that we will head to a predominantly coal-based economy have also been overdone.

Before turning to the main topic, a digression about the great conservation campaign now being mounted seems desirable. Much of the campaign appears to be a particularly blatant exercise in concocting magic potions. The pompous moralizing about habits created by national response to pre-1973 energy prices is highly inappropriate. The conservation problem is not one of moral fiber but of improper price signals. Moreover, many of the moralizers are far more guilty of causing our present energy problems than is the average U.S. citizen. It was our policymakers who initially imposed numerous restrictions on the production and use of domestic energy resources, assumed that these restrictions could easily be offset by increasing imports of cheap oil, and then failed to take actions needed to keep imported oil cheap.[3] These same policymakers have thwarted the response to price increases in imported oil: they have tightened restrictions on domestic energy, and, most notably, controls on oil prices have supplemented the controls on natural gas prices. It should also be recalled that even if conservation produces, as seems unlikely, zero or even very low energy growth, we still cannot use conservation as an excuse to prevent *all* efforts to expand energy production facilities. Replacement of worn-out operations would still be required.

In any event, the claims that conservation is the cheap solution may prove another illusion. Thus far, every other cheap solution has proven very expensive in practice, and I see no reason to bet against that record.

In particular, there is good reason to believe that the approaches taken to conservation in both the 1975 Energy Policy and Conservation Act and the president's 1977 energy message are quite unsound. The only tenet of these two approaches that seems reasonably plausible is that the consumers will benefit from better information about the energy consumption of particular durable goods.

Otherwise, efforts to prove that market failures arise in the private sector generally have a dubious basis (such as the old standby that home buyers look only at mortgage carrying costs and not at total owning costs; bankers may be guilty of this sin, but they, in turn, may be the victims of overregulation). The most convincing examples of significant market failures are those created by government—particularly energy price controls. The stress on conservation seems to be mainly an alternative to offset the effects of these price controls. The proponents who explicitly use this rationale for conservation by mandate or tax subsidy gimmicks do so because of concern over alleged undesirable income distribution effects. By their reckoning, in a free market energy prices rise, enriching the oilman, but little or no extra energy is produced.

Here, the petroleum industry must, in part, blame itself for this attitude. Industry overstatements about the impend-

ing exhaustion of our oil and gas have been employed to jus-
tify price controls. The benefits of dismantling the increasingly
complex, expensive to administer, and probably grossly ineq-
uitable system would be sufficient reason to prefer free-market
prices to price control and enforced conservation. In addition,
the potential response on both the demand and supply side
will probably be greater than expected. For the last several
years, we all have frequently encountered businessmen begging
for advice on the future of energy. They are paralyzed by lack
of clear signals from Washington or the marketplace. Free-
market pricing undoubtedly would do a great deal to end this
equivocation and cause investment in less energy-consuming
technologies. I similarly suspect free markets will elicit more
new energy production than expected. In the oil and gas realm,
the environmental advantages of these fuels, moreover, means
that any increases are boons to be welcomed enthusiastically.

Returning to coal, the political problems previously discussed interact with formidable difficulties in the economics
of coal production, processing, and use. Critics of nuclear
power have made a big point of arguing that the uncertain
financial position of electric utilities, mounting costs, and a
plethora of regulations and "public" opposition have im-
periled the nuclear industry. Until quite recently, few of
these critics recognized that similar problems arise with coal.
Fortunately, the Ford Foundation has proved that some
people can learn from their mistakes. The sensible, well-
balanced appraisal of the coal-nuclear trade-off produced by
the 1977 Ford Foundation–sponsored Nuclear Energy Policy
Study Group (the Keeny Report) has been a welcome contribution to the energy literature.[4] However, the group certainly
did not utter the last word on the subject; in particular, it
seemed to have been a bit too sanguine about coal. The rest
of this chapter develops this argument.

First, we need to take a closer look at our ignorance
about coal economics. Here, too, problems of inadequate hu-
mility are severe. Coal industry advocates are not quite sure

whether massive increases in coal utilization are a certainty or a desirable phenomenon being retarded by unwise public policies. Whatever the truth, it is quite clear that these advocates do themselves a serious disservice by relying on inadequate data on comparative resource availability. As discussed below, research on coal economics has given rise to serious questions about the long-run costs of producing and using coal. If we also consider that the potential for securing cheaper-to-utilize energy from other sources may have been underestimated, we become more cautious about the prospects for coal. Moreover, industry complaints about regulation may have been overstated. In any event, an analyst must recognize that even if the industry position were correct, policymakers may maintain existing policies. Criticism of industry overstatements, moreover, is quite different from the belief that the industry is heading for disaster. Quite the contrary, it is quite clear that lead-time considerations alone make highly unpalatable any policies that prevent a reasonable expansion of the coal industry in the next decade.

First, let us note that coal resource data are grossly inflated by the inclusion of coal whose economic viability is questionable. Table 5.1 presents my latest efforts to present adjusted figures on known recoverable reserves. Even after all the adjustments, the remaining amounts are substantial. However, there is good reason for caution in interpreting these figures.

The one proposition on which the evidence is fairly clear is that the supply of coal produced east of the Mississippi, particularly low-sulfur coal, is much less ample than a naive examination of resource figures would suggest. At least three different observers have concluded that with current technology and input costs, eastern coal output cannot be substantially expanded without recourse to more difficult mining conditions, which will cause significant increases in cost.

The final figures in Table 5.1 will represent reserves

104

TABLE 5.1

Alternative Estimates of U.S. Coal
Resources and Reserves
(billion net tons)

a.   U.S. Geological Survey Resource Figures

(1)   Estimated total identified and hypothetical
      resources remaining in the ground   3,968

(2)   Hypothetical resources with overburden
      over 3,000 feet   388

(3)   Estimated hypothetical and identified
      resources at depths less than 3,000
      feet   (1 - 2)   3,580

(4)   Estimated hypothetical resources   1,850

(5)   Total identified resources   (3 - 4)   1,730

b.   U.S. Bureau of Mines Demonstrated Reserve Base

	Underground Minable	Strip Minable	Total
Bituminous	192	41	233
Subbituminous	100	68	168
Lignite	0	28	28
Anthracite and semianthracite	7	0	7
All ranks	299	137	436

c.   U.S. Bureau of Mines Data Adjusted for
     Economic Recovery Factors

Bituminous	69	9	78
Subbituminous	24	36	60
Lignite	0	12	12
Anthracite	2	0	2
TOTAL	95	57	152

SOURCES AND NOTES:

U.S. Geological Survey: Paul Averitt, Coal Resources of
the United States, January 1, 1974, Geological Survey
Bulletin 1412, Washington, 1975, p. 14-5.

TABLE 5.1 (Cont.)

SOURCES AND NOTES: (Cont.)

U.S. Bureau of Mines: U.S. Bureau of Mines Staff, The
Reserve Base of Bituminous Coal and Anthracite for Under-
ground Mining in the Eastern United States, Information
Circular 8655, Washington, 1974; Thomas K. Matson and
Doss H. White, Jr., The Reserve Base of Coal for Underground
Mining in the Western United States, Information Circular
8678, Washington, 1975; Robert D. Thomson and Harold F. York,
The Reserve Base of U.S. Coals by Sulfur Content (In Two
Parts)--1. The Eastern States, Information Circular 8680,
Washington, 1975; Patrick A. Hamilton, D.H. White, Jr., and
Thomas K. Matson, The Reserve Base of U.S. Coals by Sulfur
Content (In Two Parts)--2. The Western States, Information
Circular 8693, Washington, 1975.

Adjusted reserves: The underground reserve figures were
adjusted by applying to the USBM figures techniques used
by the National Petroleum Council in U.S. Energy Outlook
Coal Availability, Washington, 1973. The demonstrated
reserve base of bituminous and anthracite includes coals
in seams thicker than 28 inches and subbituminous in seams
thicker that five feet. These however, are subdivided so
that those in the thinner seams can be distinguished.
Thus, generally data are given and used here on the bituminous and anthracite in seams thicker than 42 inches
(except that in western Kentucky where coal in seams thicker
than 36 inches is included) and subbituminous in seams
thicker than 10 feet. To account for the standard assumption about recovery factors in underground mining, the
numbers shown here are half the amount reported by the
Bureau. The strippable reserves are constructed by com-
bining data in the 1975 USBM reports with those in the
1971 study, Strippable Reserves of Bituminous Coal and
Lignite in the United States, Information Circular 8351.
The 1971 report started with figures on remaining strippable
resources, applied a recovery factor--generally 80 percent--
to deduce recoverable strippable resources and by collecting
data on factors such as poor coal quality and locations
where mining was infeasible (e.g., under existing cities),
deleted other portions of the reserves to produce a final
figure on economically recoverable reserves. The 1971 concept of strippable resources seems similar to that of the
demonstrated reserve base and in some cases the figures are
identical. In such cases, the 1971 figure was used to
develop the figures used here. Where the 1975 demonstrated
reserve figure differed from the 1971 remaining resource
figure, it was assumed that the proportional relationship
between resources and recoverable reserves was the same in
both years. For example, if the 1975 reserve base figure
for a state were double the 1971 strippable resources, the
1975 economically recoverable reserves were set double the
1971 figures.

recoverable at current costs only if we accept one key
assumption, namely, that coals in seams of equal thickness
have equal mining costs. This assumption contradicts what
every mining engineer argues about coal-mining economics.
Two independent studies have confirmed the insufficiency of
seam thickness as a cost predictor—an elegant statistical analysis by Martin B. Zimmerman of the Massachusetts Institute of
Technology and an exhaustive study of West Virginia mining
conditions, a study directed by Richard T. Newcomb of West
Virginia University.[5] The work done by the ICF, Inc., on coal
supply for FEA, moreover, shows that even if we adjust for
only two other determinants of costs—mine size and depth—
eastern coal supply curves are far less elastic than frequently
alleged.[6]

Moreover, the effects of depletion are reinforced by the
tendency toward rising real costs of mining even under unchanged conditions. The precipitous decline in output per
man-day starting in 1970 and sharp increases in real wages
and equipment costs have greatly increased real costs.

The critical force at work here is the growing realization
of a new generation of coal miners about the risks of their
profession. Thus far it has proven impossible to decompose
the separate effects of the numerous manifestations of these
new attitudes—such as the push for the Coal Mine Health and
Safety Act of 1969, the pressure to toughen the act and its
enforcement, the provisions of the last two union contracts,
and wildcat strikes.

The Keeny Report's contention that new technology can
reverse this trend may be correct for the very long run. However, there is a distinct danger that this long run will be so
long that success will come too late. Some support for this
view is provided by the mining technology survey that
Hittman Associates, advised by my colleagues in Mining
Engineering at Pennsylvania State University, prepared for
the Electric Power Research Institute. The report could foresee no major technical changes that could be implemented

rapidly.[7] This seems quite plausible since there is little evidence that anyone is conducting large-scale research on underground mining technology.

However, coal supplies from the northern Great Plains can apparently be increased substantially without recourse to markedly inferior reserves, and cost trends for given mining conditions in the West are apparently more favorable than in the East.[8] The big questions about the West are how much expansion the western states will tolerate and what rises in transportation costs might be produced by efforts to increase coal shipments radically. It appears that so long as coal use is limited, as it probably will be, to boilers for electric utilities and large manufacturing plants, the first problem can be resolved. The second question has thus far been too inadequately studied for reasonable conclusions to be reached. The best guess is that the transportation capacity "problem" would vanish if there were clear indications that hypothetical coal demands will actually materialize. Recall that the great coal equipment shortage evaporated when it became apparent what actual purchases would be. What the costs will be is far less clear.

Another clear proposition, already stated, is that even politicians who nominally advocate greater coal use are busily impeding, rather than promoting, such coal development. I do not claim to know whether these barriers promote legitimate social interests. However, one does get the impression that irresistible pressures have arisen to impose, without adequate reflection, the most stringent environmental regulations imaginable. Thus, a reasonable inference is that we have an excess of regulations. I would not dare attempt to measure the extent of the excess, and so will limit myself to delineating some key regulations. Most discussions of coal mining regulations stress health and safety regulations and surface mine reclamation requirements. To these may be added nationwide increases in the difficulties of securing mining rights and permits to operate mines.[9] These last problems, being less familiar, may be discussed first.

The principal barrier to coal land acquisition has been U.S. government policy. Again, excessive fears of windfall profits are exerting an excessive influence. At the 1969 sessions of this conference, Walter Mead effectively demonstrated that the Bureau of Land Management has, if anything, been overzealous in preventing windfall profits on oil and gas leases.[10] It has likewise been overzealous in the coal realm. The preferable policy goal, therefore, would be to make coal lands widely available to numerous firms able to mine coal rather than to limit lease holding to an amount the government believes is appropriate.

This last seems an unattainable and undesirable goal. How much coal is "needed" is better judged in the marketplace than by administrative decree. Wide leasing of coal rights seems more a virtue to encourage than an evil to eliminate. If large parcels of land are held by many different companies, competition in *coal* markets will be more vigorous. A tight rein on leasing gives a long head start and thus a sizable competitive advantage to present coal right holders over potential entrants. Thus, restrictive leasing policies, if anything, will have the opposite effect from that alleged by the proponents.

The restriction of leasing began in 1971 with the imposition of a Department of the Interior moratorium on leasing. The department then went through the rather protracted but sterile (in producing useful insights) exercise of providing an environmental impact statement (EIS). Although the report was typographically beautiful, it was extremely vapid, even given the low standards of EIS preparation. This process was hardly completed when the coal leasing amendments were passed—over President Ford's veto. Now President Carter's secretary of the interior has initially tended to propose what appear to be excessive environmental controls on energy development.

The problem of securing mining permits is more widespread and complex. Again, we have difficulties at the federal level. Discussions with various leading coal companies indicate that Bureau of Land Management has fallen well behind schedule in preparing the EIS required for individual mines. Everywhere problems exist in securing both mining and water discharge permits for mines on nonfederal lands: the mining permits are issued by an appropriate state agency, but federal policy governs water discharge, the enforcement of which may or may not be delegated to a state agency.

Let me next recapitulate the long-standing problems of bringing coal use into compliance with air pollution regulations. Here again the field is full of more Dr. Dulcamaras. One of my regular pastimes is reading the quarterly reports the consulting firm Pedco Environmental prepares for the Environmental Protection Agency (EPA) on stack gas scrubbing. Lately, the report has been showing that a number of scrubbers are actually operating regularly, although not necessarily effectively. However, the learning process is still slow and success far from universal. The report and other sources make clear that costs have indeed proved considerable.[11] The latest appraisals have suggested that low Btu gas-refined and solvent-refined coal are even more expensive.[12] Needless to say, this leaves me most skeptical about the latest panacea—fluidized bed boilers.

We face many other problems such as the definition of "nondegradation," pushes to require universal use of scrubbers, and protectionist measures to prevent the import of western coal into eastern coal-producing states. Ohio thwarted protectionist efforts in April 1977, but forces in the West Virginia legislature continue to mount an attack on the use of western coal in that state.

Mandating the conversion of electric power plants and large manufacturing plants to coal has to date, it is universally agreed, been unsuccessful. There is good reason to believe that the problems that have plagued the program will persist. It is even more likely that the difficulties will increase. The basic source of the failure was that the conversions were restricted by severe environmental restraints. The president has simultaneously advocated more conversions and more severe environmental constraints. In any case, mandated conversions seem one of the least efficient ways to promote coal use, and inaction seems preferable to forcing the conversions regardless of cost.

It was exceedingly difficult to reach any conclusions about all these facts before President Carter issued his energy message. Unfortunately the new dimensions added by the message have greatly complicated the analytic process. We now have to consider the possibility of a program of stimulating coal use at any cost. The premessage situation was roughly as follows:

1. The long and growing lead times on nuclear power plants severely limited the nuclear contribution in the next decade or so.
2. For numerous logistical and economic reasons, it seemed highly desirable for electric utilities and an unknown number of large industrial facilities to increase coal utilization at least until the middle 1980s.
3. Given the uncertainties about the private economics, the optimal pattern of increased coal use was unclear.
4. Because of tighter regulatory constraints on coal, it was not clear whether the "right" total amount of coal would be burned. Moreover, even if the overall use was "satisfactory," serious distortions could exist relating to who supplies the coal and who uses it.
5. By the late 1980s, a resurgence of nuclear capacity expansion might cause lessened growth or even decline of coal use.[13]

The first point is self-explanatory, so discussion can be limited to the other propositions. Most published studies suggest that for many large-scale industrial boilers already capable of burning coal and for any new large boiler being built, it would be cheaper to use coal than to use properly valued oil and gas.[14] A major source of ignorance here is the applicability of this proposition outside the electric utility sector. There are extensive data on that industry's costs and fuel use capability, but practically no information about manufacturing industry capabilities and costs. However, there is good reason (namely, the low levels of coal use) to believe that existing capabilities are small and considerable reason to fear that all too many plants are too small to benefit from the economies of scale in, say, scrubber installation or use of unit trains that help make coal use economic for electric utilities. Such limited data as have been released from FEA's survey of fuel use by large manufacturing firms suggest that few have coal use capability.[15] A critical logistical problem is that the coal-burning electric utilities are usually poorly situated for economic shipments of oil. Neither establishing a massive distribution network for heavy fuel oil nor burning middle distillates seems desirable.

The great economic issues, as might be expected from these discussions, are which users should employ coal and where should they get it. As already suggested, the manufacturing sector is the area in which the capability to use coal is most uncertain. The main coal use choices up to now have been eastern or western "compliance coal" (i.e., coals delivered with a sulfur content meeting applicable pollution requirements) and stack gas scrubbers. For reasons already outlined, many utilities and industrial users preferred the compliance coal route. Deals have been made to snatch up the shards of available, reasonably low-cost eastern coals. Even more ambitious efforts have been made to buy western coal. Substantial numbers of scrubbers have been ordered.[16]

Clearly, however, the increasing difficulties of bringing coal mines and power plants into production and the still-open question of how rapidly scrubbers can be put into *successful* operation threaten attainment of these goals. Thus, although one could be confident of a decade of growing coal use, the rate of increase remained difficult to estimate.

The conclusions about the longer-run threat of nuclear competition were based, in small part, on the fact that it seemed that by the time coal became regulated to the satisfaction of the federal government, nuclear power would appear to involve far fewer problems. A more critical consideration was that the published data on comparative costs suggested that in most of the country, nuclear power was the cheaper option. Again, nuclear critics have had the facts backward. The handling of capital cost forecasts seemed to ignore that substantially more of the required environmental controls had been embodied into nuclear plants than into coal plants. Thus, it seemed more probable that coal plant costs would rise more rapidly than comparable nuclear costs. The elaborate efforts to prove the lesser reliability of nuclear plants seemed both to give too much weight to shakedown problems and to ignore the probability that scrubbers would reduce the reliability of coal-fired plants. Finally, everyone seemed to pay little attention to the rising cost of eastern coal.

The president's energy message and 1977 legislative initiatives in coal mining and air pollution add several factors to the analysis—the effects of pressures to force greater conversion by the manufacturing industry, the best possible technology approach to air pollution control, and, possibly less critically, the imposition of national strip-mining standards. The best available technology presumably means scrubbers everywhere. The natural assumption is that such a policy combined with the pressure for more stringent strip mining regulation favors eastern coal. However, some offsets can be noted. First, some observers contend that scrubbing is cheaper and more reliable when used with low-sulfur coal.[17] Second, not only does there seem no end in sight to the rise in eastern coal prices, but the imposition of a stringent program to tax eastern underground coal producers to compensate for black lung disease damages could worsen the economics even further. Third, the plans to use western coal may in many cases be so advanced as to be irreversible.

The coal stimulus program appears unwise and probably infeasible. At a sufficient price, the private sector could undoubtedly do all that is needed to attain the objectives. The first concern is whether the price will be sufficiently low to be worth paying. Moreover, the public sector, which must approve the actions taken to increase coal use, is highly constrained in its ability to respond to the pressures to expand coal use. Thus, a second criticism of the president's approach is that he may be the victim of a particularly bad case of coal schizophrenia. He is not only seeking coal use increases that may be too large to be effected under current regulatory procedures but is also trying to complicate, rather than improve, these processes.

Since I have already stated what I believe to be the implications of these facts, my reiteration will be brief. I believe that I have made apparent the great extent to which coal schizophrenia exists, the reasons why we should be skeptical about the wisdom of such extensive controls on coal production and use, and the difficulties involved even in sustaining the growth of coal use beyond the middle 1980s. In short, I have used the case of coal as an example of why we should be much more modest in developing energy predictions and policies.

Notes

1. However, he has sought to use quite different policy tools—taxes and subsidies—to attain these goals. As my arguments below make clear, these uncritically accepted congressional goals include "conservation," increased coal use, and the imposition of greater environmental controls.

2. A characterization of Aspen chosen on the basis of my love of opera, the season in which we are meeting, and my sedentary proclivities.

3. This, of course, is an implicit endorsement of M.A. Adelman's

views on the contribution of ill-advised U.S. policies to the increase in world oil prices.

4. See the group's report, *Nuclear Power: Issues and Choices* (Cambridge, Mass.: Ballinger Publishing Co.) Since the group was chaired by Spurgeon M. Keeny, Jr., the study is referred to as the Keeny Report.

5. Zimmerman's initial work appeared in his 1975 MIT Ph.D. dissertation—"Long-Run Mineral Supply: The Case of Coal in the United States." Newcomb presented preliminary findings in a report, "The Supply of Low Sulfur Coal in Eastern Utility Markets," prepared in 1975 for a Department of Commerce Technical Advisory Committee and available in the department's library. As of spring 1977, work was in progress on the final report of the research project that provided the basis for the earlier Newcomb analysis.

6. The initial ICF study—*PIES Coal Supply Curve Methodology*, Washington, 1976—is available only at the Federal Energy Administration's National Energy Information Center. However, the methodology is outlined in ICF, *The National Coal Model: Description and Documentation* (Washington, 1976), available from the National Technical Information Service in Springfield, Virginia.

7. Hittman Associates, Inc., *Underground Coal Mining: An Assessment of Technology* (Palo Alto, Calif.: Electric Power Research Institute, and Springfield, Va.: National Technical Information Service, 1976). Some claims exist elsewhere that new haulage systems that will greatly increase productivity may emerge fairly quickly.

8. Both ICF and Zimmerman take this position. ICF, using the USBM data cited in Table 5.1 of this paper, concluded that a highly elastic supply existed of coal that met environmental regulations. This contrasts radically from the conjecture Rieber made—using earlier, less detailed data—that the supply of compliance coal in the West was more limited than many believed. See Michael Rieber, *Low Sulfur Coal: Revision of Reserve and Supply Estimates* (Urbana, Ill.: Center for Advanced Computation, University of Illinois, 1973).

9. My attention was drawn to these problems by James R. Jones, the director of Environmental Quality of Peabody Coal, who has documented the situation in papers at various industry conferences—most recently in "The Process of Developing a Western Coal Mine," presented in February 1977 to a meeting of the Colorado Mining Association.

10. See Walter J. Mead, "Federal Public Lands Leasing Policies," *Quarterly of the Colorado School of Mines* 64: no. 4 (October 1969): 181-214.

11. Pedco's report is called "Summary Report Flue Gas Desulfurization Systems." A summary of cost estimates may be found in R. L. Gordon, *Marketing Prospects for Western Coal* (Springfield, Va.: National Technical Information Service, 1977). In late 1976 the Energy Research and Development Admininstration circulated the draft of a report, "Comparing New Technologies for the Electric Utilities," which gives more recent cost data. As this chapter was being edited, the Pedco report for the first quarter of 1977 arrived and inspired an effort at more precise summary of the data—an imperfectly attainable goal given the basic complexities. Pedco lists twenty-four plants as "operational," but close examination of the data made clear immediately that this definition was quite loose and did not guarantee that the units were actively employed in pollution control. Five of the units were still undergoing shakedown; one was about to be replaced; two are each 10-megawatt units that seem to be designed for use in testing scrubber technology. Eight of the sixteen remaining units recorded significant outages during 1976 or the first quarter of 1977. This left eight units that apparently were regularly available (although one went out of service in March and had not, according to information received directly from the company, gone back into service as of mid-May). A phone survey was conducted of the operators of these eight units (one of these operators also operates two units with very high outage rates). The eight units consist of two units in the 800 megawatt range that burn high-sulfur coal, a 710-megawatt unit that burns low-sulfur coal, two 360-megawatt units that burn low-sulfur coal, a 190-megawatt unit that uses high-sulfur coal, and two units in the 60-megawatt range that also use high-sulfur coal. (High sulfur here is no less than 3.5 percent; low-sulfur, no more than 0.8 percent.) Reliability on the three largest units has been secured by resort to installation of one more scrubber module than needed to handle the gases. This allows more frequent cleaning of the units; this in turn reduces the plugging and scaling problems that have plagued earlier scrubbers. Reliability for all eight units has generally not been associated with high enough levels of sulfur removal to meet stringent criteria, such as the Environmental Protection Agency's New Source Performance Standard (NSPS), while using high-sulfur coal. The units that use low-sulfur coal, of course, do not attempt high levels of cleanup; the objectives are to remove 50-60 percent of the sulfur. The operator of one of the two largest units indicates that it is not meeting sulfur oxide regulations; the other 800-megawatt unit is meeting only state standards less stringent than NSPS. One of the three smallest units has met NSPS consistently for several years (of peaking operations); another is considered close to meeting NSPS; the operator

of the third plant was not sure how long it would take to comply with regulations less stringent than NSPS.

12. See particularly D. A. Waitzman et al., *Evaluation of Fixed-Bed Low Btu Coal Gasification Systems for Retrofitting Power Plants* (Palo Alto, Calif.: Electric Power Research Institute, and Springfield, Va.: National Technical Information Service, 1975).

13. See Gordon, *Marketing Prospects for Western Coal;* and R. L. Gordon, *Historical Trends in Coal Utilization and Supply* (Springfield, Va.: National Technical Information Service, 1976), for more extensive discussion of these arguments.

14. This oversimplifies a complex situation in which numerous factors are at work. Conversion economics are heavily affected by ability to attain economies of scale in coal transportation, handling, and emission control and by the output expectations of the unit. The cost per unit of output of investments in coal use clearly varies inversely with future utilization. A plant that will operate at high annual rates for many years can spread out the costs more effectively than a plant with a short expected life and low utilization rates. Another key factor is the extent of readiness to employ coal. This can range from availability of all the needed facilities to a situation in which the boiler is large enough to burn coal but handling facilities and space for their installation do not exist. Finally, proximity to coalfields greatly affects delivered costs.

15. FEA surveyed 822 large users of energy to determine their coal use capabilities, but few data have been released. One report indicated that of the 6,289 boilers surveyed, 947 were capable of conversion to coal. See U.S., Federal Energy Admininstration, *Implementing Coal Utilization Provisions of Energy Supply and Environmental Coordination Act* (Washington, 1976).

16. See Pedco Environmental, "Summary Report," on the scrubber orders. For summary data on coal procurement plans, see U.S., Federal Power Commission, *Status of Coal Supply Contracts for New Electric Generating Units, 1976-1985* (Washington, 1977). A listing of planned new western mines appears in John S. Corsentino, *Projects to Expand Fuel Sources in Western States* (U.S. Bureau of Mines Information Circular 8719, Washington, 1976). Corsentino's list seems to include everything about which the most tentative report exists and, in any case, does not allow for the various administrative delays that have affected even the firm commitments he reports.

17. See U.S., Department of Commerce, Technical Advisory Board, *Report on Sulfur Oxide Control Technology* (Springfield, Va.: National Technical Information Service, 1975).

6
Critical Choices
for National Energy Policy

Milton Lipton

Energy *policy* by *government* implies a resolution between the operation of the market and partly overlapping, but also partly conflicting, political objectives. Political objectives themselves are not precise. The objectives of an energy program have also to be reconciled with environmental considerations and other concerns, such as inflation and employment.

Thus, the slow and often frustrating pace at which U.S. energy policy evolves is, I believe, the almost inevitable result of the political process. We are now at a stage where the president has proposed a new National Energy Plan. Congress has yet to dispose. And I suspect that whatever is finally put into place will not be final for long. Energy policy will have to adapt to changing circumstances and perceptions. If the evolution of energy policy is to be constructive, certain critical choices must point in the right direction, and these choices, once made, must be pursued with determination.

I would single out five areas in which critical choices have to be made. First, for security reasons, a *strategic petroleum reserve*—to enable the United States to withstand interruption of insecure oil imports and hence to discourage the use of oil as a political weapon. I do not propose to dwell on this. The administration is pointing toward a billion-barrel reserve and is trying to speed up the time schedule of accumulation.

I suspect that at least some Arab producing governments are not displeased with this U.S. effort. It may in due course provide them with a counter if the cry is again raised for an embargo on production cutbacks.

Second, *domestic oil (and gas) prices* that are conducive *both* to more economical use by consumers and expanded exploration and development by producers. Whatever else, it is clear that domestic oil and gas production will be a mainstay of U.S. energy balances through the mid-1980s and beyond. This issue of price is pivotal and understandably acrimonious. I will return to it at some length.

Third, *energy conservation*. This, of course, is a sine qua non of any energy program. There is a special urgency to conservation. If there are uncertainties about elasticity of demand, can we expect price alone to do the job? But how far should government go with respect to standards or through a pains (stick) and rewards (carrot) approach?

Fourth, *coal conversion*—to shift a significant volume of energy consumption from scarce (oil and gas) to plentiful (coal) domestic resources. From an energy perspective, the choice is clear. But sharply conflicting environmental, economic, and regional interests focus precisely here. Policy in these three areas—oil and gas pricing, energy conservation, and coal conversion—will have to build a bridge to the future, to the longer-run period when alternative resources and technologies will be able to meet essential energy requirements as the petroleum age runs its course.

Fifth, *research and development* for longer-run alternatives. One can be, must be, optimistic about the future. After all, necessity is the mother of invention! But how long is the gestation period? Alternatives may not provide significant volumes of energy for fifteen or twenty years yet. In the interim, advances will have to be made that support future development. Just a few thoughts on this, and then on to the main themes of this chapter. The responsibility for technological research will almost inevitably devolve upon industry.

It has the capabilities. It offers a diversity of perspectives. It will have to have adequate incentives. Governmental policy must conduce to an industry effort that is fraught with risks and uncertainty. Capital costs are incredibly high and are compounded by inflation and interest charges over a prolonged period. Assurance as to future prices, supportive tax treatment, or even capital subventions—these should spur the considerable initiative that will be necessary if alternatives to conventional oil and gas are to be developed in the span of time still available to us. If progress is not made, energy policy could turn out to have been a bridge to nowhere.

The Price Dilemma

Today, the price exacted by OPEC is a political price. Increasingly, however, there is an awareness that continued expansion in world energy requirements and in oil consumption will be pressing on productive capacity and in time on the petroleum resource base. The difference between the CIA's doomsday scenario and the more relaxed OECD projections are differences in timing and intensity—shortages already in the early 1980s or, pray, only increasing tightness by the latter 1980s.

The point is that remaining oil reserves are becoming an increasingly scarce resource. The pressure of demand upon available supplies will mean rising *real* oil prices. Nor will renewed upward pressure on world oil prices wait upon actual shortages. The closer the perception of emerging tightness, the more intense will be the competition for preferred access, by companies and countries. At the same time, as we must look harder and farther, exploration will become more and more difficult.

On some tomorrow, *the costs imposed by nature* will become more relevant than the price exacted by OPEC. Meanwhile, however, most of the world's current oil supplies are produced at costs considerably below OPEC's political price. This is also true of incoming productive capacity, taxes aside. There is the dilemma. The difference between OPEC production costs and OPEC prices may be a political rent exacted by OPEC; it also creates an economic rent elsewhere, being the difference between historical costs and current values—hence, competing claims for shares in that economic rent.

Producers have a claim, based on the need for higher prices as an *incentive* to an expanded oil search and as a *cash flow* to fund risky exploration and costly development. Consumers, on the other hand, see no need to pay more now for oil already developed. Inflation and potential windfall profits are particularly sensitive concerns these days. Government tends to see the difference between current costs and OPEC prices as an unearned increment to which it has a claim.

Hence the dilemma of oil (and gas) price policy: how to chart a course from prices based on historical costs to incentive prices for future development?

Why Not Decontrol?

One alternative would be price decontrol. No doubt, domestic prices rising to parity with foreign oil c.i.f. would generate a huge cash flow and heighten incentives for expanded exploration. There is doubt, however, whether over the years immediately ahead the industry could mount an exploration effort commensurate with the profits thrown up by decontrol. Leasing policy alone could well be the major constraint upon domestic exploration, and that is quite another aspect of energy policy.

Withal, the potential political fallout is perhaps the most important reason for industry itself to be wary of decontrol. Decontrol, of course, does not mean going from federally regulated prices to free-market prices. It means going from price administration by U.S. government to price administration by OPEC. My point is not just a semantic one. If U.S. prices were completely freed to move in consonance with

OPEC price decisions, the U.S. oil industry would almost inevitably be perceived to be "in bed with OPEC." Every OPEC price increase would mean commensurate increases in the profitability of extant domestic production. In that event, the U.S. industry's commercial interests would be identified with OPEC's political pricing decisions. Such an impression could well have emotionally charged repercussions at a time when divestiture and tax issues are being heatedly debated.

Excess profits taxation. Sharp increases in profitability following upon decontrol would almost certainly spur efforts to impose an excess profits tax on the oil industry. Indeed, the industry itself has suggested that decontrol accompanied by an excess profits tax with plow-back provisions might be a preferred pricing policy. The case can be argued. From the industry standpoint, legislative decontrol would be a giant step forward. An excess profits tax would preclude undue profitability and, one hopes, could gradually be phased out. Meanwhile, plow-back would provide incentives for productive spending—the higher the excess profits tax rate, the greater the incentive.

To what extent would a plow-back provision spur productive spending? To what extent, competitive bonus bidding? More important, is it politically likely that an excess profits tax would be phased out? Or might an excess profits tax lead further to rate-of-return taxation? This could be critical for the future of the industry, indeed for the future of domestic exploration.

As noted, there is an urgency for expanded exploration, both in the United States and throughout the world. Looking harder and farther means more frequent and more costly failures. But that also will require more profitable successes if the effort is to carry forward. Already, however, even prospective success is constrained by increasingly stringent exploration terms imposed by host governments. And after successful discovery and development, operating terms are frequently "renegotiated." Never mind that a continuing and costly exploration effort is prerequisite to the more visible successes; the criterion of profitability tends to be a narrow one. The ring fence is tightly drawn—and not only in distant, developing countries. The United Kingdom has its Petroleum Revenue Tax, and Canada is implementing a Progressive Incremental Royalty.

Thus far the United States has avoided rate-of-return taxation. But if excess profits taxation is enacted specifically for the oil industry, it might then not be too difficult to take the next step, namely, to make excess profits the criterion for the rate of return on the lease or block. This is not meant to be confiscatory, but merely to tax away that part of the profits that is over and above what is deemed necessary to have induced the investment. In the event, however, the well-spring of exploration will have been further dammed!

Decontrol with phased-out excess profits taxation thus looks to be a pricing policy with uncertain political ramifications, which, however, may be avoided by incentive pricing (discussed below).

Incentive Pricing

An alternative pricing policy could point toward escalation of oil (and gas) prices so as (1) to ensure an incentive price for new production, and (2) to phase out "vintage" pricing and achieve a one-price system within a reasonable period. But what would be an incentive price over the years ahead is impossible to predict. In February 1970, the Cabinet Task Force on Oil Import Control visualized $2.50 per barrel as compatible with secure levels of domestic production. More recently, $7-7.50 has been suggested as a "long-run supply price," or "floor price." World oil prices, as administered by OPEC, are currently on the order of $14 c.i.f., and the longer-range cost of alternatives is often cited as $20 and up. Among these, the world price is a contemporary fact of life, at least as far as the cost of U.S. imports is concerned. The earlier, lower figures have been passed by, and the higher, projected figures are altogether conjectural.

The OPEC price per se is really quite irrelevant to the United States' energy policy. To the extent that U.S. price policy is designed to ensure domestic incentives, the United States need not in principle tie domestic prices to those set by OPEC. Over time, foreign prices could be unnecessarily high or discouragingly low in relation to domestic costs. Pragmatically, however, the present world oil price may reasonably be accepted as proxy for that illusive incentive price.

Thus, the controlled price of new oil might be escalated—to compensate for inflation *plus* an incentive increment—so as to reach parity with the c.i.f. price of world oil within a specified period, say by the early 1980s. It is at least a reasonable expectation that Saudi Arabian moderation will restrain OPEC price increases over this period when incoming productive capacity (North Slope, North Sea, etc.) will mitigate the demand for OPEC production. And if, as discussed, the world price moves ahead thereafter in real terms in response to increasingly tight supply/demand balances, continuing parity between domestic and foreign oil would not then be untoward, either economically or politically.

Meanwhile, the old oil price could be held. But the volume of established production subject to the old oil price ceiling would be progressively reduced at a rate substantially faster than the average decline rate. This would cover inflation of current production costs and would provide incentives for producers to sustain production to the maximum extent, since all production in excess of the national old oil volume would qualify for the new oil price. On this basis, a one-price system could be achieved by the early 1980s—new oil prices reaching parity with foreign oil and old oil having been phased out. This approach could avoid the political repercussions of excess profits taxation by phasing in incentive pricing and phasing out the volumes of established production subject to price ceilings. For this way we should meet at least one of the most essential requirements of pricing policy: that industry can *anticipate with confidence* the trend in domestic prices, a trend on which an expanded exploration effort would be predicated.

Administration Proposals

New oil price. Significantly, the presidential statements that heralded the administration's new energy plan made no reference to OPEC. That in itself marked quite a departure from previous rationale. OPEC was no longer the bête noire. Tightness of world oil balances was in the offing, and the United States would have to accommodate itself to higher energy costs. Details apart, a new pricing policy was proposed for new oil. Over three years, new oil prices would escalate to the present level of foreign oil prices adjusted upward for interim domestic inflation.

Roughly calculated, this means that if foreign oil c.i.f. is now somewhat over $14 per barrel and if interim inflation averages around 5 percent per annum, the new oil price would approach $17 in 1980. If OPEC prices were to increase at about the same average annual rate, the U.S. price for new oil would approximate the world price by the turn of the decade. Thereafter, the new oil price would continue to escalate with domestic inflation.

The pricing provisions of the Energy Policy and Conservation Act of 1975 had also provided for escalation at the rate of domestic inflation *plus* a 3 percent per annum incentive factor. Incongruously, escalation was applied to an average composite price of domestic crude, and this resulted in a roll-back, instead of an increase, in upper-tier (i.e., new) oil prices. Now, however, it is proposed to escalate the price of new oil directly. Although an inflation adjustment makes sense as an offset to the industry's rising production unit costs—wages, prices of oil field equipment, etc.—the added incentive adjustment has been lost. This adjustment would offset a rising trend in costs of exploration and development, which is likely to reflect the costs exacted by nature more than those imposed by inflation.

If an expanded exploration effort means looking harder and farther, the costs of finding and developing the new reserves that must support future production must be expected to be in a rising trend. Accordingly, legislating a firm statutory rate of escalation for new crude prices for at least a minimum period of years might be considered, in order to subsume both anticipated inflation and to provide incentive increases, as discussed above.

Old oil prices. Lower-tier and upper-tier prices are also to escalate from current levels in line with domestic inflation. To the extent that actual producing costs do not go up in proportion to inflation, particularly for lower-tier production, per barrel producing margins are likely to improve somewhat on most established production. However, applying the same percentage inflation adjustment to lower-tier, upper-tier, and new oil means that actual price differentials at the wellhead will widen. Furthermore, the introduction of a new tier for new oil suggests the possibility at least that there could in time be further vintaging of subsequent production. If so, the multitier price structure would not only be perpetuated, but expanded.

Wellhead equalization tax. The administration proposes that the crude-cost basis of domestic refining, and hence consumer product prices, be brought up quickly to the level of incremental cost (i.e., foreign crude prices c.i.f.). The mechanism is a wellhead equalization tax that raises lower-tier prices paid by refiners up to upper-tier prices in two stages and that then raises lower-tier and upper-tier prices to the new oil price level. In effect, consumers are being told that they must begin to pay full incremental world oil prices for petroleum products. For the present, the equalization tax is a device whereby producers are denied "windfalls" on established, lower-cost crude, even though refiners and consumers will be charged world prices.

Intended or not, the proposed crude-oil price equaliza-

tion tax could provide a mechanism for more flexible adjustment than heretofore of wellhead prices. For the future,
reductions in the equalization tax would enable new oil
prices to be increased if added exploration incentives were
deemed necessary. Similarly, lower-tier or upper-tier prices or
both can be increased if enhanced cash flow is deemed necessary. Unlike past regulation, such future increases in wellhead
prices need not result in higher consumer costs and thus
provoke the political issues that have hitherto been involved
in crude price adjustments.

Any future shift in crude-oil production revenues from
the government's equalization-tax take to the producers'
wellhead price receipts would presumably be predicated on
the course of events such as the magnitude, cost, and relative
success of the industry's exploration effort, and such as the
emerging costs of development, particularly in frontier areas,
and consequent cash flow needs. Realistically, too, much
could depend on how the equalization tax revenues are being
disposed. To the extent that such revenues are bound up for
specified purposes and vested with sectarian or regional
interests, it would be more difficult to cede higher margins to
crude oil producers.

For many reasons, it might well be preferable to com-
mingle equalization tax revenues within the government's
general funds. In the first instance, that would permit reductions in overall budgetary deficits and hence in borrowing,
easing inflationary pressures precisely at the time when other
aspects of energy policy are inevitably fueling the inflationary spiral. Subsequently, shifts from the equalization-tax take
to wellhead prices might be less fraught with conflicting
interests.

On balance, the pricing proposals of the administration's
energy plan seem to be a mixed bag. Prices to consumers
would be substantially increased, largely reflecting incremental
costs and thus more consistent with conservation objectives.
This, in itself, is a major step forward. A new oil price is pro-

jected at appreciably higher levels than heretofore. The well-head prices of both new and established production would escalate with inflation, but multiple-tier pricing is perpetuated. The constraints of a composite price are thrown off, but an incentive increment has been lost in the process. The wellhead equalization tax provides a mechanism to effect future wellhead price increases—for an added incentive or for enhanced cash flow or for both. But whether this occurs will depend to a considerable extent on how the disposition of tax revenues engenders continuing claims for those tax dollars.

As already noted, legislated escalation of new crude prices for at least a specified number of years, to offset both anticipated inflation *and* to provide incentive increases, could dispel much of the uncertainty that surrounds the administration's pricing proposals. Phasing out lower-tier and upper-tier production could be conducive to a simplified price structure.

Energy Conservation

As noted at the outset of this chapter, energy conservation is essential to the administration's plan or to any effective energy policy. Growth in total energy consumption is now projected at around 2.5 percent per annum through 1985, compared with 3 percent "without plan." By the mid-1980s, the administration's proposals visualize a slowing in the growth rate to below 2 percent.

The plan's targets thus represent a significant reduction in energy consumption. Savings would come roughly to the equivalent of 2 million barrels of oil daily over the administration's "without plan" projection. Nevertheless, the proposed energy program still implies *continuing increases in per capita energy consumption.* Significantly higher energy costs are projected. Users will largely have to pay incremental costs. That this will affect energy consumption is clear; to

TABLE 6.1

U.S. Energy Demand, 1976
and Projections for 1985

(Millions of barrels daily oil equivalent)

	1985 Carter Administration		1976
	With Plan	Without Plan	1976
Total Demand	46.4	48.3	37.0
Residential/ Commercial	15.2	16.1	13.8
Industry	20.6	21.4	13.7
Transportation	10.5	10.8	9.5
Of which: Electricity[1]	15.5	16.3	10.5

NOTE:

May not sum to totals in all cases owing to rounding.

(1) Gross energy inputs to electricity generation.

what extent—the elasticity of demand?—is less clear.

Interestingly, the administration expects little additional savings in gasoline consumption beyond those already projected on the basis of existing automotive mileage standards. Auto taxes, rebates for new cars, and higher gasoline taxes are buttresses to the program, but they may not survive persistent opposition except in truncated version.

The projected energy savings are about equally divided between the residential/commercial and industrial sectors (see Table 6.1). Within the residential/commercial sector, the bulk of the net energy savings is expected in electricity consumption. Indeed, savings in this sector's use of electricity account for almost all of the projected reduction in total electric power consumption. These savings would be effected by means of household appliance standards, restructuring of electric utility rates to discourage consumption during peak demand periods and to penalize instead of reward incremental consumption, tax credits for insulation, and the use of solar energy.

Within the industrial sector, energy consumption in 1985 is expected to be held to 20.6 mmb/doe—800,000 b/d, or 4 percent, below the "without plan" projection. Conservation in this sector already seems to have been substantial over the past several years. Although further savings would be progressively more difficult to achieve, the 1985 target appears to be well within the scope of measures set out in the plan. To achieve the targeted fuel balances in industry, notably sharply increased use of coal, would be quite a different matter (of which more later).

Success in slowing the growth trend in energy consumption to 1985 will hinge significantly on the elimination of waste and profligate consumption and on improvements in technology and processes that are most readily affected. After that, when the savings have been largely achieved, energy growth could well resume at rates above those of the years leading into 1985. Here, as in other key aspects of administration energy policy, the plan is essentially a bridging action over the next eight years or so; its purpose is to achieve a posture from which the United States can move forward, but with the shape of the future still not at all defined.

Given historical patterns of inefficient energy consumption, substantial conservation ought to be attainable. Progressively higher energy prices and price expectations should be conducive to lesser and more efficient use of energy. Similarly, tax incentives should be conducive to the investment necessary to accomplish conservation and at the same time improve the efficiency with which energy is used in the U.S. economy.

Details apart, the administration is likely to pursue energy conservation aggressively, adding penalties or inducements or both as deemed necessary in the light of future trends. Here, at least, the administration's energy perspectives and conservationist ethic look to be reasonably consistent.

TABLE 6.2

Fuel Balances in the Industrial and
Electric Utility Sectors, 1976
and Projections for 1985

(Millions of barrels daily oil equivalent)

| | 1985 Carter Administration | | 1976 |
	With Plan	Without Plan	1976
Industry	20.6	21.4	13.7
Oil	4.0	7.0	3.2
Natural Gas	4.5	4.5	4.4
Electricity	7.1	7.2	4.2
Coal	5.0	2.7	1.9
Electric Utilities	15.5	16.3	10.5
Oil	1.3	2.0	1.6
Natural Gas	0.5	0.9	1.5
Coal	8.3	8.2	4.9
Nuclear	3.8	3.7	1.0
Hydro/other	1.7	1.7	1.5

NOTE:

May not sum to totals in all cases owing to rounding.

Coal Conversion

If energy conservation is essential to effective energy
policy, coal conversion is pivotal. Previous coal projections
were for a difficult billion tons annually by 1985. Now, the
coal production target is on the order of 1.25 billion tons.
Significantly, the additional 0.25 billion tons of coal (2.5
mmb/doe) is expected to be absorbed largely in the industrial
sector, displacing oil. In that event, coal consumption in the
industrial sector would shoot up to 5 mmb/doe by 1985,
almost twice the previously projected 1985 level and about
2.5 times the 1976 figure (see Table 6.2). Oil consumption in
the industrial sector under the plan would be reduced 3
mmb/d below previously projected levels and would be only
800,000 b/d higher than in 1976. Coal would then account
for 25 percent of total industrial energy and exceed the contribution of oil.

In the electric utility sector, coal would account for over half of total fuel consumption in 1985, although there is no projection of further displacement of oil and natural gas. In effect, coal requirements for electric power would have been met out of previously projected production. As noted, additional coal production under the plan is assumed to move into industrial end uses. Projected reductions in oil and natural gas use by electric utilities under the plan largely reflect lower electric power requirements rather than further displacement by coal or nuclear power.

The coal is expected to come from both western strip mining of low-sulfur coal and eastern pit mining of high-sulfur coal. The major focus had been previously on western coal development, but the plan envisages a considerable expansion of eastern mining. This shift in focus may ease somewhat the environmental and transportation problems associated with accelerated strip mining of western coal; burning eastern high-sulfur coal, however, obviously adds to the environmental problems.

How to spur conversion to coal? The plan utilizes a stick and carrot approach. On the one hand, it prohibits new oil and natural gas electric power installations and the burning of these fuels by extant installation with dual burning facilities; it also imposes a progressive tax on oil and natural gas used by electric utilities and industry. On the other hand, there are tax credits or rebates of oil and gas user taxes paid for investment in conversion and stack-gas scrubbing facilities.

Coal and the Environment

There are awesome difficulties confronting the Carter coal conversion policy, not in principle but in practice. Strip mining of western low-sulfur coal involves inevitable conflicts, or at least trade-offs, with environmental considerations. Contour restoration, preservation of agricultural land, park and wilderness area protection—all these could seriously inhibit the pace of coal development, and clean water issues will impinge on mining potential as well as possible coal-slurry transportation.

Coal consumption is similarly confronted with innumerable environmental difficulties. Clean air issues have already, and could increasingly, set barriers to electric power generation at or close to mine sites.[1] Stack-gas scrubbing may be a sufficient recourse for certain qualities of coal and in certain areas. But is it the whole answer? And what will it cost?

The plan states specifically that the "attainment and maintenance of the environmental goals set out in the Clean Air Act, the Federal Water Pollution Control Act, and the National Environmental Policy Act are high national priorities. The Administration intends to achieve its energy goals without endangering the public health or degrading the environment." But if coal conversion, the heart of the administration plan, lags seriously—either on the production or the consumption side—because of environmental barriers, how will potentially conflicting objectives of policy be reconciled? This could be the single most crucial question for future administration policy. There is as yet no clue how the priorities will be assessed.

Notes

1. For example, delays due to environmental and regulatory problems were major factors forcing the cancellation last year of the proposed 3,000-megawatt Kaiparowits coal-fired plant in southern Utah.

Appendix A:
Participants in the 1977
Rocky Mountain Energy
Economics Institute

Chairman and moderator:
Bob Burch

Papers and addresses delivered by:

Edward W. Erickson
Professor of Economics
North Carolina State University
Raleigh, North Carolina

Herbert S. Winokur, Jr.
Vice President
Pennsylvania Company
Los Angeles, California

James W. McKie
Professor of Economics
University of Texas
Austin, Texas

Joel Darmstadter, Economist
Resources for the Future
Washington, D.C.

Richard L. Gordon
Professor of Economics
Pennsylvania State University
University Park, Pennsylvania

John F. O'Leary, Administrator
Federal Energy Administration
Washington, D.C.

Milton Lipton
Executive Vice President
W. J. Levy Consultants Corporation
New York, New York

L. G. Rawl, Executive Vice President
EXXON Company USA
Houston, Texas

Pierre Wack, Chief Economist
Shell International
    Petroleum Co., Ltd.
London, England

Registrants:

Bernhard J. Abrahamsson
Industrial Economics Division
University of Denver Research
    Institute
Denver, Colorado 80208

Linn F. Adams
Vice President and
    Regional Manager
Champlin Petroleum Company
P.O. Box 1257
Englewood, Colorado 80110

James E. Akins
2904 Garfield Terrace
Washington, D.C.

The Rocky Mountain Energy Economics Institute was held at The Gant, Aspen, Colorado, June 26-29, 1977.

133

Philip F. Anschutz, Owner
The Anschutz Corporation
1110 Denver Club Building
Denver, Colorado 80202

George T. Ballou
Standard Oil Co. of California
225 Bush Street
San Francisco, California 94104

Thomas C. Barger
Consultant
2685 Calle Del Oro
La Jolla, California 92037

Dr. James A. Barlow, Jr.
Barlow & Haun, Inc.
139 West Second
Casper, Wyoming 82601

S. F. Bird
Exploration & Production Mgr.
Mobil Oil Corporation
P.O. Box 5444
Denver, Colorado 80217

W. T. Blackburn, Partner
Vaughey, Vaughey & Blackburn
1650 Denver Club Building
Denver, Colorado 80202

Robert T. Blakely, Vice President
Morgan Stanley & Co. Incorporated
1251 Avenue of the Americas
New York, New York 10304

J. W. Bruskotter, Associate Dir.
Marathon Oil Company
Denver Research Center
P.O. Box 269
Littleton, Colorado 80122

Bob Burch
1077 Race Street, Suite 204
Denver, Colorado 80206

Edward J. Cahill
Standard Oil Co. of California
225 Bush Street, Room 1119
San Francisco, California 94105

Annon M. Card
Senior Vice President
Texaco Inc.
135 East 42nd Street
New York, New York 10017

Professor John A. Carver, Jr.
University of Denver College of Law
200 West 14th Avenue
Denver, Colorado 80204

Collis P. Chandler, Jr., President
Chandler & Associates, Inc.
1401 Denver Club Building
Denver, Colorado 80202

Norman R. Chappell
Minister Counsellor (Energy)
Canadian Embassy
1746 Massachusetts Avenue, N.W.
Washington, D.C. 20036

Sherman H. Clark
S. H. Clark Associates
1100 Alma Street
Menlo Park, California 94025

Dr. E. Anthony Copp
Solomon Brothers
41st Floor
1 New York Plaza
New York, New York 10004

C. W. Corbett
Energy Consultant
1015 Metrobank Building
475−17th Street
Denver, Colorado 80202

Dr. James S. Cross
Vice-President, Pol. Dev.
American Petroleum Institute
2101 L Street, N.W.
Washington, D.C. 20037

R. Gale Daniel, Director
Planning for the Syn. Fuels Div.
Atlantic Richfield Company
515 South Flower Street
Los Angeles, California 90071

David G. Davidson, President
Edgington Oil Company, Inc.
2400 East Artesia Boulevard
Long Beach, California 90805

Warren B. Davis, Chief Economist
Gulf Oil Corporation
P.O. Box 1166
Pittsburgh, Pennsylvania 15230

Bernard Delapalme
Société Nationale Elf Aquitaine
7, rue Nelaton
75739 Paris Cedex 15, France

George S. Dibble, Jr.
Vice-President, Comm. & Pub. Rel.
Husky Oil Company
P.O. Box 380
Cody, Wyoming 82414

Commissioner Ronald D. Doctor
California Energy Resources
    Conservation & Development
    Comm.
1111 Howe Avenue
Sacramento, California 95825

Charles R. Dodson
351 Ridgecrest Drive
Santa Barbara, California 93108

Theodore R. Eck, Senior Economist
Standard Oil Company (Indiana)
200 East Randolph Drive-MC 2905A
Chicago, Illinois 60680

Harry Gevertz
El Paso Natural Gas Company
P.O. Box 1492
El Paso, Texas 79978

Wayne Gibbens, President
Mid-Continent Oil & Gas Assn.
1800 K Street, N.W., Suite 620
Alexandria, Virginia 22308

Honorable Assemblyman
    Terry Goggin
State of California
State Capitol—Room 2176
Sacramento, California 95814

Ray Golden
Solomon Brothers
1 New York Plaza, 41st Floor
New York, New York 10004

Barry Good
Morgan, Stanley and Company
1251 Avenue of the Americas
New York, New York 10020

Maury Goodin,
    Chairman of the Board
Petroleum Information Corp.
P.O. Box 2612
Denver Colorado 80201

George Gray
Assistant to U.S. Representative
    Patricia Schroeder
1767 High Street
Denver, Colorado 80218

Mariano Gurfinkel
Petroven
P.O. Box 169
Caracas, Venezuela, South America

John Guy, Committee Coordinator
National Petroleum Council
601 Commonwealth Building
1625 K Street, N.W.
Washington, D.C. 20006

Harold D. Hammar
The Chase Manhattan Bank, N.A.
One Chase Manhattan Plaza
New York, New York 10015

Donald A. Henriken
Atlantic Richfield Company
515 South Flower Street, No. 4919
Los Angeles, California 90071

John H. Hertog, Vice President
Operations
Burlington Northern
176 East Fifth Street
St. Paul, Minnesota 55101

Edward R. Heydinger
Marathon Oil Company
539 South Main Street
Findlay, Ohio 45840

W. H. Hopper, President
Petro-Canada
P.O. Box 2844
Calgary, Alberta, Canada T2P 2M7

Robert Baynes Horton
The British Petroleum Co. Ltd.
Britannic House, Moor Lane,
London, EC2Y 9BU, England

William H. Kelly
Manager Corporate Economics
Planning and Economics Dept.
United Gas Pipeline Company
P.O. Box 1478
Houston, Texas 77001

Christopher P. King, President
BP North America, Inc.
620 Fifth Avenue
New York, New York 10020

David J. Kull
Farmers Union Central Exchange, Inc.
P.O. Box 126
Laurel, Montana 59044

J. B. Ladd, President
Ladd Petroleum Corporation
830 Denver Club Building
518—17th Street
Denver, Colorado 80202

James C. Langdon, Jr.
Akin, Gump, Strauss, Hauer & Feld
1155—15th Street, N.W., Ste. 1100
Washington, D.C. 20005

Craig Liske, Assistant to
    U.S. Representative Tim Wirth
9485 W. Colfax
Denver, Colorado 80215

W. L. Lurie
Executive Vice-President
International Paper Company
220 East 42nd Street
New York, New York 10017

Charles K. McArthur
Utah International Inc.
550 California Street
San Francisco, California 94104

Malcolm McDuffie
Mohawk Petroleum Corporation, Inc.
550 South Flower Street
Los Angeles, California 90071

Donald J. McNutt, President
Douglas Oil Co. of California
P.O. Box 2500
Costa Mesa, California 92626

Larry D. McVay
Engineering Staff Specialist
Standard Oil Company (Indiana)
200 East Randolph Drive-MC 2905A
Chicago, Illinois 60680

Charles Maxwell
Cyrus J. Lawrence Inc.
115 Broadway
New York, New York 10006

Dr. Edward Mitchell
Professor of Economics
University of Michigan
Ann Arbor, Michigan

Ken Monroe
Executive Director
Colorado-Nebraska Division
Rocky Mountain Oil and Gas Assn.
950 Petroleum Club Building
Denver, Colorado 80202

K. E. Montague, President
General Crude Oil Company
P.O. Box 2252
Houston, Texas 77001

Rush Moody, Jr.
Vinson & Elkins
1701 Pennsylvania Ave., N.W.
Suite 1120
Washington, D.C. 20006

Warren A. Morton
Morton Brothers, Inc.
254 North Center Street
Casper, Wyoming 82601

O. Neathery, III
Planning Manager
Mobil Oil Corporation
P.O. Box 5444
Denver, Colorado 80217

Marshall Nichols
National Petroleum Council
601 Commonwealth Building
1625 K Street, N.W.
Washington, D.C. 20006

James E. Nielson, President
Husky Oil Company
P.O. Box 380
Cody, Wyoming

A. A. Phillips
Division Exploration Manager
Exxon Company USA
P.O. Box 120
Denver, Colorado 80201

Dr. James Ramsey
Professor of Economics
New York University
New York, New York

R. L. Rayl
Regional Manager
Phillips Petroleum Company
1000 Security Life Building
Denver, Colorado 80202

Donald F. Rodgers
International Brotherhood of
    Teamsters
25 Louisiana Avenue, N.W.
Washington, D.C. 20001

Roger W. Sant
al Dir'iyyah Institute
1925 North Lynn Street, Suite 1120
Arlington, Virginia 20009

G. Henry M. Schuler
Vice-President
Government Relations &
    Public Affairs
Champlin Petroleum Company
P.O. Box 9365
Fort Worth, Texas 76107

Milton F. Searl
Electric Power Research Institute
P.O. Box 10412
Palo Alto, California 94304

A. B. Slaybaugh, Vice President
Continental Oil Company
1755 Glenarm Place
Denver, Colorado 80202

Don S. Smith, Commissioner
Federal Power Commission
825 North Capitol Street
Washington, D.C. 20426

J. William Sorensen
Managing Partner
Boettcher & Company
828—17th Street
Denver, Colorado 80202

Arthur O. Spaulding
Vice-President and General Manager
Western Oil and Gas Association
609 South Grand Avenue, Suite 910
Los Angeles, California 90017

Dr. Michael Telson
Staff Economist
House Ad Hoc Committee on Energy
Room 321 Cannon Office Building
Washington, D.C. 20515

M. Ray Thomasson
McCormick Oil and Gas
1204 Tenneco Building
Houston, Texas 77002

Clarke Watson
Watson & Associates
1429 Larimer Square
Denver, Colorado 80202

Roy Whisenhunt, General Manager
Energy Resources Department
Texaco Inc.
P.O. Box 2100
Denver, Colorado 80201

E. L. Williamson, President
The Louisiana Land and
    Exploration Co.
P.O. Box 60350
New Orleans, Louisiana 70160

Marc F. Wray, Vice-President
Planning, Development &
    Diversified Business
General Crude Oil Company
P.O. Box 2252
Houston, Texas 77001

John H. Young
Attorney at Law
903 Esperson Building
Houston, Texas 77002

Appendix B:
Summary of the National
Energy Plan

Conservation

In the transportation sector, the Plan proposes the following major initiatives to reduce demand:

—a graduated excise tax on new automobiles with fuel efficiency below the fleet average levels required under current legislation: the taxes would be returned through rebates on automobiles that meet or do better than the required fleet averages and through rebates on all electric automobiles;

—a standby gasoline tax, to take effect if total national gasoline consumption exceeds stated annual targets; the tax would begin at 5 cents per gallon, and could rise to 50 cents per gallon in 10 years if targets were repeatedly exceeded by large or increasing amounts; the tax would decrease if a target were met; taxes collected would be returned to the public through the income tax system and transfer payment programs; States would be compensated for lost gasoline tax revenues through sources such as the Highway Trust Fund;

Reprinted from *The National Energy Plan*, Executive Office of the President, Energy Policy and Planning (Washington, D.C.), 1977, pp. XV-XXIII.

—fuel efficiency standards and a graduated excise tax
and rebate system for light-duty trucks;

—removal of the Federal excise tax on intercity buses;

—increase in excise tax for general aviation fuel, and
elimination of the existing Federal excise tax prefer-
ence for motorboat fuel;

—improvement in the fuel efficiency of the Federal
automobile fleet, and initiation of a vanpooling program for Federal employees.

To reduce waste of energy in existing buildings, the Plan
proposes a major program containing the following elements:

—a tax credit of 25 percent of the first $800 and 15 per-
cent of the next $1,400 spent on approved residential
conservation measures;

—a requirement that regulated utilities offer their residential customers a "turnkey" insulation service, with
payment to be made through monthly bills; other fuel
suppliers would be encouraged to offer a similar service;

—facilitating residential conservation loans through
opening of a secondary market for such loans;

—increased funding for the current weatherization program for low-income households;

—a rural home conservation loan program;

—a 10 percent tax credit (in addition to the existing
investment tax credit) for business investments in ap-
proved conservation measures;

—a Federal grant program to assist public and non-
profit schools and hospitals to insulate their buildings;

—inclusion of conservation measures for State and local
government buildings in the Local Public Works Program.

The development of mandatory energy efficiency
standards for new buildings will be accelerated. In addition,
the Federal Government will undertake a major program to
increase the efficiency of its own buildings.

The Plan proposes the establishment of mandatory minimum energy efficiency standards for major appliances, such as furnaces, air conditioners, water heaters, and refrigerators.

The Plan proposes to remove major institutional barriers to cogeneration, the simultaneous production of process steam and electricity by industrial firms or utilities, and to provide an additional 10 percent tax credit for investment in cogeneration equipment. Encouragement will also be given to district heating, and the Energy Research and Development Administration (ERDA) will undertake a study to determine the feasibility of a district heating demonstration program at its own facilities.

To promote further industrial conservation and improvements in industrial fuel efficiency, an additional 10 percent tax credit for energy-saving investments would be available for certain types of equipment (including equipment for use of solar energy) as well as conservation retrofits of buildings.

The Plan also contains a program for utility reform, with the following elements:

- —a phasing out of promotional, declining block, and other electric utility rates that do not reflect cost incidence; declining block rates for natural gas would also be phased out;
- —a requirement that electric utilities either offer daily off-peak rates to customers willing to pay metering costs or provide a direct load management system;
- —a requirement that electric utilities offer customers interruptible service at reduced rates;
- —a prohibition of master metering in most new structures;
- —a prohibition of discrimination by electric utilities against solar and other renewable energy sources;
- —Federal authority to require additional reforms of gas utility rates;
- —Federal Power Commission (FPC) authority to require interconnections and power pooling between utilities even if they are not now subject to FPC jurisdiction, and to require wheeling.

Oil and Natural Gas

Government policy should provide for prices that encourage development of new fields and a more rational pattern of distribution; but it should also prevent windfall profits. It should promote conservation by confronting oil and gas users with more realistic prices, particularly for those sectors of the economy where changes can be made without hardship. To promote these ends, the Plan proposes a new system for pricing oil and natural gas.

The proposal for oil pricing contains the following major elements:

- —price controls would be extended;
- —newly discovered oil would be allowed to rise over a 3 year period to the 1977 world price, adjusted to keep pace with the domestic price level; thereafter, the price of newly discovered oil would be adjusted for domestic price increases;
- —the incentive price for "new oil" would be applicable to oil produced from an onshore well more than 2½ miles from an existing well, or from a well more than 1,000 feet deeper than any existing well within a 2½ mile radius; the incentive price would be applicable to oil from Federal offshore leases issued after April 20, 1977;
- —the current $5.25 and $11.28 price ceilings for previously discovered oil would be allowed to rise at the rate of domestic price increases;
- —stripper wells and incremental tertiary recovery from old fields would receive the world price;
- —all domestic oil would become subject in three stages to a crude oil equalization tax equal to the difference between its controlled domestic price and the world oil price; the tax would increase with the world price, except that authority would exist to discontinue an increase if the world price rose significantly faster than the general level of domestic prices;

—net revenues from the tax would be entirely returned to the economy; residential consumers of fuel oil would receive a dollar-for-dollar rebate, and the remaining funds would be returned to individuals through the income tax system and transfer payment programs;

—once the wellhead tax is fully in effect, the entitlements program would be terminated, along with certain related activities, but would be retained on a standby basis.

The proposal for natural gas pricing contains the following major provisions:

—all new gas sold anywhere in the country from new reservoirs would be subject to a price limitation at the Btu equivalent of the average refiner acquisition cost (before tax) of all domestic crude oil;

—that price limitation would be approximately $1.75 per thousand cubic feet (Mcf) at the beginning of 1978; the interstate-intrastate distinction would disappear for new gas;

—new gas would be defined by the same standards used to define new oil;

—currently flowing natural gas would be guaranteed price certainty at current levels, with adjustments to reflect domestic price increases;

—authority would exist to establish higher incentive pricing levels for specific categories of high-cost gas, for example, from deep drilling, geopressurized zones and tight formations;

—gas made available at the expiration of existing interstate contracts or by production from existing reservoirs in excess of contracted volumes would qualify for a price no higher than the current 41.42 per Mcf ceiling; gas made available under the same circumstances from existing intrastate production would qualify for the same price as new gas;

—the cost of the more expensive new gas would be allo-

cated initially to industrial rather than residential or
commercial users;

—Federal jurisdiction would be extended to certain synthetic natural gas facilities;

—taxes would be levied on industrial and utility users of
oil and natural gas to encourage conservation and
conversion to coal or other energy sources.

The Plan contains the following additional proposals for
oil and natural gas:

—to encourage full development of the oil resources of
Alaska, Alaskan oil from existing wells would be subject to the $11.28 upper tier wellhead price and would
be treated as uncontrolled oil for purposes of the entitlements program; new Alaskan oil finds would be
subject to the new oil wellhead price;

—production from Elk Hills Naval Petroleum Reserve
would be limited to a ready reserve level at least until
the west-to-east transportation systems for moving the
surplus Alaskan oil are in place or until California
refineries have completed a major retrofit program to
enable more Alaskan oil to be used in California;

—the Outer Continental Shelf Lands Act would be
amended to require a more flexible leasing program
using bidding systems that enhance competition, to
assure a fair return to the public, and to assure full
development of the OCS resources;

—shale oil will be entitled to the world oil price;

—the guidelines established by the Energy Resources
Council in the previous administration would be replaced by a more flexible policy; projects for importa-
tion of liquefied natural gas (LNG) should be analyzed
on a case-by-case basis with respect to the reliability of
the selling country, the degree of American dependence the project would create, the safety conditions
associated with any specific installation and all costs
involved; imported LNG would not be concentrated in

any one region; new LNG tanker docks would be prohibited in densely populated areas;
—Federal programs for development of gas from geopressurized zones and Devonian shale would be expanded;
—the Administration hopes to eliminate gasoline price controls and allocation regulations next fall; to maintain competition among marketers, it supports legislation similar to the pending "dealer day in court" bill;
—as part of the extension of oil and natural gas price controls, the Administration would urge that independent producers receive the same tax treatment of intangible drilling costs as their corporate competitors;
—a Presidential Commission will study and make recommendations concerning the national energy transportation system.

To provide relative invulnerability from another interruption of foreign oil supply, the Strategic Petroleum Reserve will be expanded to 1 billion barrels; efforts will be made to diversify sources of oil imports; contingency plans will be transmitted to the Congress; and development of additional contingency plans will be accelerated.

Coal

Conversion by industry and utilities to coal and other fuels would be encouraged by taxes on the use of oil and natural gas.

The Plan also contains a strong regulatory program that would prohibit all new utility and industrial boilers from burning oil or natural gas, except under extraordinary conditions. Authority would also exist to prohibit the burning of oil or gas in new facilities other than boilers. Existing facilities with coal-burning capability would generally be prohibited from burning oil and gas. Permits would be required for any conversion to oil or gas rather than to coal. By 1990, virtually no utilities would be permitted to burn natural gas.

While promoting greater use of coal, the Administration will seek to achieve continued improvement in environmental quality. A strong, but consistent and certain, environmental policy can provide the confidence industry needs to make investments in energy facilities. The Administration's policy would:

- —require installation of the best available control technology in all new coal-fired plants, including those that burn low sulfur coal;
- —protect areas where the air is still clean from significant deterioration;
- —encourage States to classify lands to protect against significant deterioration within 3 years after enactment of Clean Air Act amendments;
- —require Governors to announce intent to change the classification of allowable air quality for a given area within 120 days after an application is made to construct a new source in that area;
- —require States to approve or disapprove the application within 1 year thereafter.

Further study is needed of the Environmental Protection Agency's policies allowing offsetting pollution trade-offs for new installations. A committee will study the health effects of increased coal production and use, and the environmental constraints on coal mining and on the construction of new coal-burning facilities. A study will also be made of the long-term effects of carbon dioxide from coal and other hydrocarbons on the atmosphere.

The Administration supports uniform national strip mining legislation.

An expansion is proposed for the Government's coal research and development program. The highest immediate priority is development of more effective and economic methods to meet air pollution control standards. The pro-

gram will include research on:
- —air pollution control systems;
- —fluidized bed combustion systems;
- —coal cleaning systems;
- —solvent refined coal processes;
- —low Btu gasification processes;
- —advanced high Btu gasification processes;
- —synthetic liquids technology;
- —coal mining technology.

Nuclear Power

It is the President's policy to defer any U.S. commitment to advanced nuclear technologies that are based on the use of plutonium while the United States seeks a better approach to the next generation of nuclear power than is provided by plutonium recycle and the plutonium breeder. The U.S. will defer indefinitely commercial reprocessing and recycling of plutonium. The President has proposed to reduce the funding for the existing breeder program, and to redirect it toward evaluation of alternative breeders, advanced converter reactors, and other fuel cycles, with emphasis on nonproliferation and safety concerns. He has also called for cancellation of construction of the Clinch River Breeder Reactor Demonstration Project and all component construction, licensing, and commercialization efforts.

To encourage other nations to pause in their development of plutonium-based technology, the United States should seek to restore confidence in its willingness and ability to supply enrichment services. The United States will reopen the order books for U.S. uranium enrichment services, and will expand its enrichment capacity by building an energy-efficient centrifuge plant. The President is also proposing legislation to guarantee the delivery of enrichment services to any country that shares U.S. nonproliferation objectives and accepts conditions consistent with those objectives.

To resolve uncertainties about the extent of domestic uranium resources, ERDA will reorient its National Uranium Resources Evaluation Program to improve uranium resource assessment. The program will also include an assessment of thorium resources.

The United States has the option of relying on light-water reactors to provide nuclear power to meet a share of its energy deficit. To enhance the safe use of light-water reactors:

  —the Nuclear Regulatory Commission (NRC) has already increased the required number of guards at nuclear plants and the requirements for the training that guards receive;

  —the President is requesting that the NRC expand its audit and inspection staff to increase the number of unannounced inspections and to assign one permanent Federal inspector to each nuclear power plant;

  —the President is requesting that the Commission make mandatory the current voluntary reporting of minor mishaps and component failures at operating reactors;

  —the President is requesting that the Commission make mandatory the current voluntary reporting of minor mishaps and component failures at operating reactors;

  —the President is requesting that the NRC develop firm siting criteria with clear guidelines to prevent siting of nuclear plants in densely populated locations, in valuable natural areas, or in potentially hazardous regions.

The President has directed that a study be made of the entire nuclear licensing process. He has proposed that reasonable and objective criteria be established for licensing and that plants which are based on a standard design not require extensive individual licensing.

To ensure that adequate waste storage facilities are available by 1985, ERDA's waste management program has been expanded to include development of techniques for long-term storage of spent fuel. Also, a task force will review

ERDA's waste management program. Moreover, improved methods of storing spent fuel will enable most utilities at least to double their current storage capacity without constructing new facilities.

Hydroelectric Power

The Department of Defense (Corps of Engineers), together with other responsible agencies, will report on the potential for installation of additional hydroelectric generating capacity at existing dams throughout the country.

Nonconventional Resources

America's hope for long-term economic growth beyond the year 2000 rests in large measure on renewable and essentially inexhaustible sources of energy. The Federal Government should aggressively promote the development of technologies to use these resources.

Solar Energy

Solar hot water and space heating technology is now being used and is ready for widespread commercialization. To stimulate the development of a large solar market, a tax credit is proposed. The credit would start at 40 percent of the first $1,000 and 25 percent of the next $6,400 paid for qualifying solar equipment. The credit would decline in stages to 25 percent of the first $1,000 and 15 percent of the next $6,400. The credit would be supported by a joint Federal-State program of standards development, certification, training, information gathering, and public education. Solar equipment used by business and industry would be eligible for an additional 10 percent investment tax credit for energy conservation measures.

Geothermal Energy

Geothermal energy is a significant potential energy source. The tax deduction for intangible drilling costs now available for oil and gas drilling would be extended to geothermal drilling.

Research, Development and Demonstration

An effective Federal research, development and demonstration program is indispensable for the production of new energy sources. The Federal Government should support many research options in their early stages, but continue support into the later stages only for those that meet technical, economic, national security, health, safety, and environmental criteria. Research and development should be accompanied by preparation for commercialization so that successful projects can rapidly be put to practical use.

Additional research, development and demonstration initiatives are proposed, with emphasis on small, dispersed and environmentally sound energy systems.

An Office of Small-Scale Technologies would be established to fund small, innovative energy research and development projects. The office would enable individual inventors and small businesses to contribute to the national energy research and development effort.

Information

A three-part energy information program is proposed. A Petroleum Production and Reserve Information System would provide the Federal Government with detailed, audited data on petroleum reserve estimates and production levels. A Petroleum Company Financial Data System would require all large companies and a sample of small firms engaged in crude oil or natural gas production to submit detailed financial information to the Federal Government. Data required from integrated companies would permit evaluation of the performance of their various segments by providing vertical accountability. An Emergency Management Information System would provide the Federal and State governments with information needed to respond to energy emergencies.

Competition

Effective competition in the energy industries is a matter of vital concern. The Under Secretary for policy and evaluation in the proposed Department of Energy would be responsible for making certain that policies and programs of the Department promote competition. Although at this time it does not appear necessary to proceed with new legislation for either horizontal or vertical divestiture of the major oil companies, their performance will be monitored. The proposed information program would greatly assist that effort.

A present anomaly in the availability of the tax deduction for intangible drilling costs within the oil industry would be removed as part of the program for extending oil and natural gas price controls.

Emergency Assistance for Low-Income Persons

Existing emergency assistance programs are deficient in assisting low-income persons to meet sharp, temporary increases in energy costs due to shortages or severe winters. A redesigned program will be completed promptly and submitted to the Congress.